Herbert Cushing Tolman, Karl Pomeroy Harrington, Hermann Steuding

Greek and Roman Mythology

Herbert Cushing Tolman, Karl Pomeroy Harrington, Hermann Steuding

Greek and Roman Mythology

ISBN/EAN: 9783744772440

Printed in Europe, USA, Canada, Australia, Japan

Cover: Foto ©ninafisch / pixelio.de

More available books at **www.hansebooks.com**

The Students' Series of Latin Classics

Greek and Roman Mythology

BASED ON

STEUDING'S GRIECHISCHE UND RÖMISCHE MYTHOLOGIE

BY

KARL POMEROY HARRINGTON

PROFESSOR OF LATIN IN THE UNIVERSITY OF NORTH CAROLINA

AND

HERBERT CUSHING TOLMAN

PROFESSOR OF GREEK IN VANDERBILT UNIVERSITY

LEACH, SHEWELL, AND SANBORN
BOSTON   NEW YORK   CHICAGO
1897

Norwood Press
J. S. Cushing & Co. — Berwick & Smith
Norwood Mass. U.S.A.

PREFACE

In adapting Steuding's Griechische and Römische Mythologie to the needs of American students, two aims have been kept steadily in view: first, that the genesis and development of the myths should be clearly set forth; secondly, that the text should be supplemented by a generous supply of references to some of the most useful literary passages illustrative of the subjects in hand. Therein lie whatever claims this little book has to a place among the various attractive text-books that have recently appeared upon the same subject. It is not a dictionary, perhaps not even a reference book; but rather an attempt to furnish within small compass a consistent and systematic exposition of the development of mythology and religion among the Greeks and Romans.

With a view to the practical convenience of all classes of students likely to use the book, it has seemed wisest as a rule to spell the proper names in the way in which they commonly occur in English literature and in classical dictionaries. Mere transliterations of Greek epithets, and the like, are, of course, not Latinized; but where a Latin form exists it has usually been preferred. While perfect consistency in form is unattainable on these principles, it is believed that such consistency is less desirable than the advantages otherwise gained.

As a guide to proper pronunciation, the quantities of all the long vowels have been marked in the index, and, in the text, in names printed in italic or full-faced type.

Grateful acknowledgments are hereby accorded to the various scholars that have contributed towards perfecting the form and accuracy of the book: especially to Professor Francis Kingsley Ball of the University of North Carolina, for his many valuable suggestions and his painstaking care in reading the proof; to Dr. H. F. Linscott of the University of North Carolina, for reading part of the proof; and to Professor E. M. Pease, editor-in-chief of the series, for his wise criticism and help at every stage of the work.

KARL POMEROY HARRINGTON.
HERBERT CUSHING TOLMAN.

JANUARY, 1897.

BRIEF BIBLIOGRAPHY

Fiske, J., Myths and Myth-makers, Boston, 1881.

Frazer, J. G., The Golden Bough, New York and London, 1894.

Furtwängler, A., Meisterwerke der griechischen Plastik, Leipzig, 1893 *sq*. English edition by Eugénie Sellers, London, 1895 *sq*.

Gruppe, O., Die griechischen Culte u. Mythen in ihrer Beziehungen zu den orientalischen Religionen, Leipzig, 1887 *sq*.

Harrison and Verrall, Mythology and Monuments of Ancient Athens, London and New York, 1890.

Jacobi, Ed., Handwörterbuch der griech. u. röm. Mythologie, Coburg and Leipzig, 1835.

Lang, A., Myth, Ritual, and Religion, London, 1887; article on "Mythology" in Encyclopædia Britannica, 9th ed., vol. 17, p. 135.

Maass, Ernst, Orpheus : Untersuchungen zur griechischen, römischen, altchristlichen Jenseitsdichtung und Religion, Munich, 1895.

Mannhardt, W., Antike Wald- und Feldkulte, Berlin, 1877; Mythologische Forschungen, Strassburg, 1884.

Mayer, M., Die Giganten und Titanen in der antiken Sage und Kunst, Berlin, 1887.

Meyer, E. H., Indogermanische Mythen, Berlin, 1883 *sq*.

Müller, H. D., Mythologie der griechischen Stämme, Göttingen, 1857–1859.

Müller, K. O., Prolegomena zu einer wissenschaftlichen Mythologie, Göttingen, 1825.

Müller, Max, Chips from a German Workshop; Science of Religion, London, 1873; Science of Language, 7th ed., London, 1873.

Overbeck, J., Geschichte d. griech. Plastik, 4th ed., Leipzig, 1894; Griechische Kunstmythologie, in progress, Leipzig, 1871 sq.

Pater, W., Greek Studies, London, 1895.

Preller, L., Griechische Mythologie, Berlin, 1854; 4th ed. by C. Robert, 1887 sq.; Römische Mythologie, Berlin, 1858; 3d ed. by H. Jordan, 1881-1883.

Rohde, E., Psyche, Freiburg i. B., 1890.

Roscher, W. H., Studien zur vergleichenden Mythologie der Griechen und Römer, Leipzig, 1873 sq.; Studien zur griechischen Mythologie und Kulturgeschichte vom vergleichendem Standpunkte, Leipzig, 1878 sq.; Ausführliches Lexikon der griechischen und römischen Mythologie, Leipzig, 1884 sq.

Sittl, K., Archäologie der Kunst (Vol. VI. of Müller's Handbuch d. klass. Altertumswissenschaft), Munich, 1895.

Stengl, P., Chthonischer und Totenkult, Leipzig, 1895.

Töpffer, J., Attische Genealogie, Berlin, 1889.

Tylor, E. B., Primitive Culture, London, 1871; Anthropology, New York, 1881.

Welcker, F. G., Griechische Götterlehre, Göttingen, 1862.

Whitney, W. D., Oriental and Linguistic Studies, series, New York, 1874.

Wilamowitz-Moellendorf, U. von, Euripides's Herakles, Vol. I., Berlin, 1889.

The most complete grouping and discussion of all the literature that appeared on the subject of Greek and Roman mythology during the years 1876-1885 is made by A. Preuner in Bursian's Jahresbericht, Vol. 25; all works on Greek mythology that appeared during 1886-1890 are similarly treated in Vol. 26, by Friedrich Back; and summaries of still later mythological literature have been made by O. Gruppe in the same periodical in 1894 and 1895.

TABLE OF CONTENTS

A. THE ORIGIN OF MYTHS

	PAGE
1. The Soul and the Worship of the Dead, §§ 1–9	1
2. The Divinities of Nature, §§ 10–14	10
3. The Worship of the Gods, §§ 15–19	13

B. THE GREEK GODS

I. THE DIVINITIES OF THE HEAVENS.
  1. Representatives of the Phenomena of the Thunderstorm: Zeus (Giants, Cyclops), §§ 20–31; Hephaestus, §§ 32, 33; Prometheus, § 34; Athena (Erinyes, Gorgons, Graeae), §§ 35–42 16
  2. W... divinities: Harpies, § 43; Wind gods, § 44; ...ies, §§ 45–48 34
  3. Divinities of Light: Apollo, §§ 49–53; Helios, § 54; Hera, §§ 55, 56; Artemis, §§ 57, 58; Hecate, §§ 59, 60; Selene, §§ 61, 62; Stars, § 63; Eos, § 64; Iris, § 65 38

II. THE DIVINITIES OF THE EARTH, § 66.
  1. Fire goddess: Hestia, § 67 52
  2. Water divinities: Lesser Sea divinities, §§ 68–71; Poseidon, §§ 72–75; River gods, § 76; Centaurs, §§ 77, 78; Sileni, § 79; Nymphs, § 80 52
  3. Divinities of Growth, § 81: Satyrs, § 82; Pan, §§ 83, 84; Dionysus, §§ 85–93; Demeter and Core, §§ 94–98; Gaea, § 99 63

TABLE OF CONTENTS

III. THE DIVINITIES OF THE LOWER WORLD.   PAGE
   1. Divinities of Death: Hades, §§ 100, 101   75
   2. Divinities of Sickness and Healing: Aesculapius,
      §§ 102, 103   77

IV. PERSONIFICATIONS, § 104   78
   1. The Divinities of Love, Social Intercourse, Order, and
      Justice: Aphrodite, §§ 105–109; Eros, §§ 110, 111;
      Charites, §§ 112, 113; Muses, § 114; Horae and
      Themis, § 115   79
   2. The Divinities of War and Strife: Ares, §§ 116, 117 . 87
   3. The Divinities of Destiny: Moerae, § 118; Nemesis,
      § 119; Tyche, §§ 120, 121   89

C. THE GREEK HEROES

   1. Thebes: Cadmus, § 123; Antiope, § 124; Niobe,
      § 125   93
   2. Argolis: Io, § 126; Danaüs, § 127; Perseus, § 128;
      Tantalus, §§ 129–131   96
   3. Corinth: Sisyphus, § 132; Bellerophontes, § 133 . .   103
   4. Laconia: Dioscuri, § 134; Helen, § 135   105
   5. Hercules, §§ 136–149   106
   6. Theseus, §§ 150–158   117

CYCLES OF MYTHS.
   1. Meleager and the Calydonian Hunt, §§ 159, 160 . .   122
   2. The Argonauts, §§ 161–166   124
   3. The Theban Cycle, §§ 167–174   128
   4. The Trojan Cycle, §§ 175–186   134

D. THE ROMAN GODS, § 187

I. DIVINITIES NOT REDUCED TO A UNIFORM CONCEPTION.
   (1) Souls: Genii, Junones, Lares, Manes, Lemures,
       Larvae, §§ 188, 189   145
   (2) Spirits of Activity: Indigetes, § 190   146

II. DEIFIED FORCES OF NATURE, AND DIVINITIES CLOSELY
RELATED TO SPIRITS OF ACTIVITY.
    PAGE
(1) Spring goddesses, § 191; River gods, § 192; Neptunus, § 193 147
(2) Janus, §§ 194, 195; Vesta, § 196; Volcanus, § 197; Saturnus, Consus, and Ops, § 198 149
(3) Divinities of Fruitfulness: Faunus, § 199; Silvanus, Liber, Vertumnus, § 200; Fauna, Feronia, § 201; Flora, Pales, § 202; Diana, § 203 153
(4) Mars, §§ 204, 205; Quirinus, § 206 157

III. DIVINITIES OF THE HEAVENS: Juppiter, §§ 207–210; Juno, §§ 211, 212 160

IV. DIVINITIES OF DEATH: Orcus, Mania, Lara, § 213 . . 165

V. PERSONIFICATIONS, § 214 166

VI. DIVINITIES ORIGINALLY FOREIGN, §§ 215–218 167

INDEX 171

GREEK AND ROMAN MYTHOLOGY

---oo⦂o⦂oo---

A. THE ORIGIN OF MYTHS

1. The Soul and the Worship of the Dead

1. Even in the earliest stages of civilization, before the human mind devoted any very careful study to its external surroundings, the instinct of self-love impelled man to investigate the processes that he saw going on in himself and in creatures like himself. Sickness and death were the first to attract his attention; for they interrupt the course of everyday life. Then dreams — which sometimes, especially when attended by the nightmare, seem exceedingly real — suggested the existence of beings which, though imperceptible to the senses, can yet affect human life, now agreeably, and again disagreeably. These beings, accordingly, came to be regarded as the authors of certain phenomena, which were apparently inexplicable in any other way. · Therefore, supported by the universal inborn desire for the continuance of personal life after death, there grew up a belief in the existence of the souls (ghosts) of the dead. Closely related to this was the belief in elves or fairies, — a superstition which even yet, in races that have remained in the lowest stages of development, appears to be about the only general form of faith extending beyond mere physical sensations.

2. Although the Greeks and Romans in historic times had long since passed beyond the earlier stages of development, yet all their ideas with regard to sickness, death, and the continued existence of the soul, were based entirely upon the views of that early period. Naturally, in process of time, a later series of conceptions, based upon quite different hypotheses, was intermingled with the more primitive ones; but at all events those seem to be among the most ancient which grew out of the principal characteristics which the dead had possessed in life. As with most of the other Indo-European nations, burial was their earliest form of laying away the dead; and the grave itself was regarded as the dwelling place of the departed one, who still enjoyed an existence in bodily form. It was customary to bury food and drink, implements and weapons, with the dead; and originally a man's favorite wife and those slaves that during his life he had considered essential to his welfare were compelled to share death and the grave with him. Thus, as late as the Iliad, Achilles at the funeral of Patroclus is represented as killing twelve Trojan youths, probably with the idea that he shall in that way make their souls the slaves of his friend in the next world. After a while the offering of animals was substituted for that of human beings; yet the gladiatorial combats also, which were a customary feature of funeral games at Rome, were evidently a kind of substitution for the sacrifice of slaves or prisoners. There was a belief also that the dead as well as the living could enjoy such prize contests.

3. Of course it was necessary to replenish the supply of food and drink occasionally; consequently the **worship of the dead** at the tomb consisted chiefly in the repeated offering of the means of subsistence. The custom grew up of doing this on the anniversaries of the birth and death of the departed one, and during the general celebrations in honor of the dead. Such occasions at Athens were the *Nekysia* or *Nemeseia* on the 5th day of the month Boëdromion (September–October), and the *Chytroi* on the 13th of Anthesterion (February–March); at Rome, the *Lemūria* on the 9th, 11th, and 13th of May, and the *diēs parentālēs*, which were celebrated towards the close of the older Roman year, beginning with the 13th of February, and ending with the *Fērālia* on the 21st. Souls punished neglect by sending sickness or death; and so by the Greeks they were called Keres, *i.e.* destroyers; by the Romans, Larvae or Lemures, specters. Therefore, to guard against the evil influence of these dreaded beings, and to prevent their return into their former dwellings, all such rites were resorted to as were commonly employed in the effort to avoid any other evil.

4. At this stage in the development of the idea souls were believed to retain the form and physical peculiarities of the dead body. It was thought that by an offering of fresh blood (which is lacking after the heart ceases to beat) they could be temporarily called back to life, and could answer questions, a supposition out of which were developed **necromancy** and the oracles of the dead. In connection with these oracles there appeared at a later period in Greece oneiromancy also (divination by dreams ascribed to the deities of the lower world). For it was believed that the god or demigod living in the depths of the earth appeared personally in a dream to those that slept in his sanctuary (*incubātiō*), and gave them his counsel. Almost as ancient as these conceptions seems to be the idea that when the soul departed from the body it assumed animal form. The serpent especially, a creature of noiseless and rapid movements, which often lives in the ground, was commonly regarded as the soul in brute form; and among other forms attributed to souls, at least by the Greeks, were those of bats, birds, and, later, butterflies.

5. From the observation that a dead body gradually crumbles away, the belief at length became common that **the dead are not body, but spirit**; and as people saw that the cessation of life's activity was coincident with the expiration of the last breath, they came in time to look upon the breath itself as the fundamental principle of life, *i.e.* as the soul, — a fact that is demonstrated by the double signification of ψυχή, *anima*, "breath," and similar words. Therefore souls that had left the body were imagined to be airy; but still, on account of an intermixture of the earlier idea, there was attributed to them a human or animal form. So they were conceived of sometimes as shadowy figures (σκιαί, *umbrae*), or smoke-like phantoms (εἴδωλα, *simulācra*, *imāginēs*), sometimes as tiny, winged creatures with human form.

6. At Rome, in connection with the worship of the dead, the older conceptions endured. In Greece also, where they had ceased to prevail generally about the beginning of the seventh century B.C., they spread again everywhere at a comparatively late period, under the influence of the Boeotians and Dorians, who had not advanced beyond the corresponding stage of development. In Homer, on the other hand, such ideas can be recognized only in isolated allusions, since in his time the later doctrine was already accepted among the Achaians and Ionians, whose view he represented. Simultaneously among these peoples, from the ordinary characteristics of every grave, there had grown up the idea of a common place of **abode for souls**, subterranean, naturally, but not accessible to human beings through the medium of prayers and offerings, an abode separated from the world above by impassable rivers, such as the Styx ('the hated'), Acheron ('river of woe'), Cocytus ('river of lamentation'), Pyriphlegethon ('stream of fire'), and Lethe ('forgetfulness') from which the dead drank forgetfulness.

7. As soon as the dead had been covered with earth, their souls, lingering on the bank of the Styx or the Acheron, were ferried across by the boatman Charon. As pay for this service he received an *obolus* (a small coin worth $3\frac{1}{2}$ cents), which customarily was laid under the tongue of the deceased. Once down in the **lower world**, the dead, according to Homer's belief, lived a gloomy, empty, shadowy sort of life. Their previous tastes and occupations were, indeed, unchanged; but their life was without consciousness and the power to effect any actual results. A few individuals, however, who were especially loved or hated by the gods, retained consciousness and sensation, that they might be rewarded or punished for their deeds done upon earth. From this realm of death there could be no return; to this end the three-headed dog Cerberus kept watch at the entrance, which the ancients believed they had discovered in various places, *e.g.* at Cichyrus in Thesprotia, Pheneüs in Arcadia, on the promontory Taenarum in Laconia, and at Lake Avernus near Cumae. Charon, too, carried nobody back over the Styx. (The divinities that rule in the lower world are discussed in §§ 100–103.)

8. Upon another conception, of later origin, rests the idea of **Elysium**, — the field of arrival, or of those that have gone over (*cf.* ἐλήλυθα), — which was supposed to be at the western boundary of the earth, on Oceanus, not in the lower world. For, without the necessity of first suffering death, many of the heroes and heroines especially dear to the gods, begotten from mortals, or otherwise nearly allied to divine beings, were carried off to this abode, there to enjoy a blessed, godlike life of pleasure. With the later poets the 'Isles of the Blessed' take the place of this. But not until after the fifth century B.C., with the growth of a belief in a retributive justice, was there developed the idea of a tribunal of the dead. According to this idea an abode either in Elysium, the home of the blessed, or in **Tartarus**, the gloomy place of punishment, the deepest abyss of the lower world, is assigned to the dead by Minos, Rhadamanthus, and Aeacus, the decision in each case depending on the character of the life lived on earth.

9. Among the Romans, in later times, the souls of the dead were commonly designated by the flattering term **Mānēs**, *i.e.* 'the Pure,' 'the Good,' or were called, in general, *inferī*, 'those of the nether world.' Each family worshiped especially the spirits of its own ancestors, as the *deī īnferūm parentum*, or the *deī parentēs* or *patriī*. Very strictly, too, did they preserve a conscientious observance of all the precepts applying to solemn

burial; and even after cremation had become the usual custom, the old usages, which had been based on the idea of interment, were never essentially altered. However, the conception of a common abode for souls never thoroughly prevailed at Rome; and, on account of the similarity of death to sleep, the later epitaphs seem to indicate a belief that the dead slumbered forever in the grave, and were free from care, peaceful and happy. (*Cf.* Divinities of Death, § 213.)

Styx: Homer, Il. xiv. 271, Od. x. 513: —

> ἔνθα μὲν εἰς Ἀχέροντα Πυριφλεγέθων τε ῥέουσιν
> Κώκυτός θ᾽, ὅς δὴ Στυγὸς ὕδατός ἐστιν ἀπορρώξ.

Ovid, Met. iii. 76, Ars Amat. i. 635, ii. 41; Vergil, Geor. iv. 480; Milton, Par. L. ii. 577: —

> Abhorred Styx, the flood of deadly hate;
> Sad Acheron, of sorrow, black and deep;
> Cocytus, named of lamentations loud
> Heard on the rueful stream; fierce Phlegethon,
> Whose waves of torrent fire inflame with rage.

Pope, Thebais i. 411: —

> For by the black infernal Styx I swear,
> (That dreadful oath which binds the thunderer);

Ode on St. Cecilia's Day 90: —

> Tho' fate had fast bound her
> With Styx nine times round her.

Shak., Troilus and Cressida v. 4, 20; Spenser, F. Q. i. i. 37.

Acheron: Homer, Od. x. 513; Vergil, Aen. vi. 295; Spenser, F. Q. i. v. 33; Milton, Par. L. ii. 577.

Cocytus: Vergil, Geor. iii. 38, iv. 479, Aen. vi. 297, 323; Pope, Thebais i. 419: —

> Whose ghost yet shivering on Cocytus' sand
> Expects its passage to the further strand.

Shak., Titus Andronicus ii. 3, 236: —

> As hateful as Cocytus' misty mouth.

Spenser, F. Q. i. i. 37.

Pyriphlegethon: Ovid, Met. v. 544; Vergil, Aen. vi. 551;
Pope, Ode on St. Cecilia's Day 50: —

> Th' infernal bounds,
> Which flaming Phlegethon surrounds.

Lethe: Ovid, Trist. iv. 1, 47: —

> Utque soporiferae liberem si pocula Lethes,
> Temporis adversi sic mihi sensus hebet.

Vergil, Aen. vi. 705, 714; Tennyson, In Memoriam xliii.: —

> And in the long harmonious years
> (If Death so taste Lethean springs)
> May some dim touch of earthly things
> Surprise thee ranging with thy peers.

Milton, Par. L. ii. 583: —

> Lethe, the river of oblivion, rolls
> Her wat'ry labyrinth, whereof who drinks
> Forthwith his former state and being forgets,
> Forgets both joy and grief, pleasure and pain.

Shak., King Henry IV. pt. ii. v. 2, 72, King Richard III. iv. 4, 250;
Spenser, F. Q. i. iii. 36.

Charon: Vergil, Aen. vi. 298: —

> Portitor has horrendus aquas et flumina servat
> Terribili squalore Charon.

Pope, Dunciad iii. 19: —

> Taylor, their better Charon, lends an oar.

Swift, A Quibbling Elegy on Judge Boat: —

> Our Boat is now sail'd to the Stygian ferry,
> There to supply old Charon's leaky wherry;
> Charon in him will ferry souls to Hell;
> A trade our Boat has practised here so well.

Shak., Troilus and Cressida iii. 2, 11.

Cerberus: The conception of a dog guarding the lower world is very old. In the Rig Veda there are frequent allusions to the offspring of Sarama, the bitch of Indra, who conduct to the other world those whom Yama summons. In Vendidad, xiii. 9 of the Avesta, dogs are represented as sentinels of the other world. In the Funeral hymn, another portion of which is cited below, the dogs appear in one stanza in a hostile attitude, in the others as kind to those whom they conduct. They are mentioned in Rig Veda vii. 55, 2–3, x. 14, 10. Rig Veda x. 14: —

10. Run past the two dogs, offspring of Sarama, four-eyed, brinded, by a straight path. Then go unto the fathers, kindly noticing, who with Yama revel in common revel.

11. These dogs which are thine, the guardians, O Yama, four-eyed, guarding the path, men-beholding, to them give over this (man), O king, for well-being and to him extend weal.

Vergil, Geor. iv. 483 : —
        Tenuitque inhians tria Cerberus ora.

Ovid, Her. ix. 93, Met. iv. 449, ix. 185 ; Milton, L'Allegro 1 : —
        Hence loathèd Melancholy
        Of Cerberus and blackest Midnight born.

Shak., King Henry IV. pt. ii. ii. 4, 182, Troilus and Cressida ii. 1, 37 ; Spenser, F. Q. i. v. 34.

Elysium: Hesiod, Works and Days 170 ; Pindar, Ol. ii. 67 *sq.*; Vergil, Geor. i. 38, Aen. vi. 637 *sq.*; Shak., Cymbeline v. 4, 117 : —
        More sweet than our blessed fields;

Two Gentlemen of Verona ii. 7, 38, Twelfth Night i. 2, 4.

Tartarus: Homer, Od. xi. *passim*; Ovid, Fast. iv. 605; Vergil, Aen. vi. 577.

Minos: Homer, Il. xiii. 450; Ovid, Met. viii. 6 *sq.*, Her. xv. 347 ; Vergil, Aen. vi. 432 ; Hyginus, Fab. xl.-xliv.

Aeacus: Homer, Il. xxi. 189; Ovid, Met. vii. 471 *sq.*; Horace, Od. ii. 13, 22 ; Hyginus, Fab. lii.

Manes: The following is translated from the tenth book of the Rig Veda. Although the hymn is acknowledged to be much later than other portions of the Rig Veda, yet the stanzas given are undoubtedly of very ancient date. They will be interesting to show the early ancestor-worship among the Indo-European peoples.

Yama, father of mankind and king of departed souls, waits to receive the dead into his kingdom of light. Roth has made an interesting comparison between the Sanskrit Yama and the Avestan Yima. Yama is the son of Vivasvant; so Yima. Yama is called "Gatherer of peoples"; so Yima in Vendidad ii. 21 of the Avesta makes a "gathering of men." Yama is the first mortal to reach heaven and gathers the blessed to himself. Rig Veda x. 14 : —

1. The one gone forth over the great heights, the one pointing out the path to many, | the son of Vivasvant, the gatherer of peoples, Yama the king, him worship with an oblation.

2. Yama was the first to find a refuge for us: this (heavenly) pasture is not to be taken from us : | whither our fathers of old have gone, thither the children are going along their pathways.

7. Go forth, go forth by the ancient paths whither our fathers of old have gone. | Both kings exhilarated with the sweet oblation, Yama and heavenly Varuṇa thou wilt see.

8. Meet with the fathers, with Yama, with the reward (in store for thee) in highest heaven. | Leaving what is sinful come back home: possessing full life meet a (new) body.

9. Go away (ye mourners), go apart and disperse from here. The fathers have made this place for him, | adorned with days, with waters, with nights. Yama gives to him a resting-place.

2. Origin and Development of the Conception of the Divinities of Nature

10. The inborn impulse in man to endeavor to comprehend the causal connection of all phenomena observed by him could not long confine itself to the events that concern his own person. Before long he began to consider also the world of nature, in which he lives, and whose influence he feels. A child attributes the property of life to the objects surrounding him, as soon as they appear to exert any active influence. So, by one who is as yet but a simple child of nature, everything that exerts any power is regarded as endowed with life, because activity, in connection with its own peculiar motion and productiveness, appears to him as the chief characteristic of a living being. Soon, however, he perceives that the apparent activity belonging to things without life is frequently produced by living beings hidden from view. Through this experience he reaches the point of presupposing in general for every exercise of power a living being as the author, upon whose particular form and fashion he decides according to the nature of the operation of the force in each case. Thus fancy gradually peopled the whole world of nature in which man lived — so far as activity, motion, and productiveness were observed — with a countless number of living beings, which may be called **divinities of nature**. These, like the beings which the human imagination had in a similar manner created out of souls, could not be directly perceived by the senses, and so the two kinds of supersensual beings were easily compared with each other. The natural result was that the peculiarities of the beings developed from souls, having been already determined, were transferred to the divinities of nature.

11. Now, if the observed exercise of power in any process of nature is mightier and of longer duration than can come from an ordinary human being or animal, the presupposed author is exalted above the measure of man or beast, as regards might and duration of life. Moreover, according as this power appears hostile or friendly, strong or gentle, active or passive, towards mankind, so in each case there is attributed to the being whose action is supposed to be thus manifested a friendly, or an unfriendly disposition, and masculine or feminine gender.

12. These divinities of nature, whose identity was preserved among the Greeks in the multitudes of river gods, centaurs, nymphs, nereids, satyrs, etc., were essentially different from the gods proper. For, during the stage of belief in such divinities, an exhibition of a given force is not attributed to some being that always produces similar results in similar objects; but, rather, every object of nature exhibiting signs of the activity of life is supposed to be inhabited and preserved by a special divinity of its own. The transition from belief in the minor divinities to **belief in gods** always follows first in the sphere in which strict distinctions of place and object are not noticed, *i.e.* in the case of the divinities that work in the heavens and the air. For, in the case of storms, winds, clouds, sun, and moon, it cannot be decided whether the same phenomenon is constantly repeated, or whether various, yet similar, phenomena follow each other.

13. With the uniting of individual families into races and states, the divinities that have in a certain sense been independently created by each family can for the first time rise to the dignity of gods generally recognized and clearly conceived of as individual beings by the mass of the people. For, until then, the real identity of various individual conceptions cannot be discovered; and, on the other hand, it is not until this stage of progress that the spirit of an ancestor of a ruling family can become the hero of a race.

14. When, at length, in the progress of civilization and culture, the superiority of spiritual power over everything physical is recognized, the gods become more and more spiritualized. As they are stripped of the sensual characteristics of animals or human beings, they gradually develop more or less completely into purely spiritual deities, defenders of morals and the moral laws, which have meanwhile grown up among mankind under divine direction. Such beings as these were the gods of the Greeks and the Romans in the best period in the life of those peoples. Not until the gods are recognized in this light can the independent **deification of abstract ideas** begin; but after such recognition it is no longer a necessary requisite for the creation of a personality that there should be an activity perceptible by the senses. It cannot, however, be denied that there is a sort of spiritual action in such figures as Ate ('infatuation'), Apate ('deception'), Dike ('justice'), Themis ('law'), Irene ('peace'), and Nike ('victory'), which are found even in the oldest Greek poets.

3. Origin of the Worship of the Gods

15. Since man can conceive of all supernatural beings only as superior personalities made after his own image, he endeavors to influence them in the same manner as in the case of powerful human beings. He shows them his reverence by approaching them in humble posture, with purified body and clean raiment. He begs for their favor, and, if they are displeased, for their indulgence or pardon. He presents them with the best of what he himself possesses, in order to insure for himself their good will, to express his thanks for benefits received, or to atone and make expiation for any offence toward them.

16. Such is the origin of the three principal **forms of worship,** — purification, prayer, and sacrifice. To express humble reverence and submissiveness one would either actually cast himself down upon the ground ($\pi\rho o\sigma\kappa\nu\nu\epsilon\hat{\iota}\nu$, *supplicāre*), or at least stretch out his upturned palm toward the abode, or the image, of the divinity. Men sometimes confined themselves with chains or bands, that thus they might surrender themselves entirely helpless into the divine hands. For the same reason, at a later period, in the performance of every holy act they wound bands ($\tau\alpha\iota\nu\iota\alpha\iota$, *taeniae*, *vittae*) around their heads, just as they did around the sacrificial animals and other objects consecrated to the gods. The word *religiō*, indeed, signifies properly that relation of being bound which one sustains toward a divinity,— the obligation or duty which one feels toward him.

17. All **purification** (*lustrātiō*, from *luō*, καθαρμός) relates originally to the body; and water is the chief requisite in connection with it. Purification was, accordingly, considered especially necessary in case of a murder attended with bloodshed, or of touching a dead person, though the idea of deliverance from guilt was not at first associated with it. For this purpose water from the sea or from a spring was preferred, because neither of these remains impure. **Prayer** is properly a simple request, the effect of which, however, can be heightened by the addition of a promise or a vow (εὐχή, *vōtum*). Prescribed formulas were employed only because their success seemed to have shown that they, more than other words, were efficacious in influencing the gods to grant the desire expressed.

18. Anything that is likely to please a divinity may be offered as a gift (ἀνάθημα). **Appropriate gifts** would be, first, such objects as are used in acts of worship or for the adornment of a temple; secondly, such as possess a particular value for the person offering them. But the most common of all gifts to the gods was the offering of food and drink. Such offerings consisted of all the things that please the taste of man himself; for originally physical enjoyment was presupposed even in the case of the gods. At a later time, by the burning of the offering, the vapor and smoke, at least, exhaling an agreeable odor, were made to ascend to the realm of the celestials.

19. Finally, as men gave expression to their will by signs or words, the effort was made to discover the will of the gods in **omens** (τέρατα, *ostenta*), such as lightning, rainbows, eclipses of the sun and moon, and the flight of birds, or to learn it from significant words and sounds (φῆμαι, κληδόνες, ōmina). From the omens were developed in Greece the sign oracles of Zeus; in Italy, the *auspicia* and the whole science of the augurs. From the words and sounds arose the oracular responses of Apollo. The inspection of the liver and other entrails of slain sacrificial animals grew up later out of the general requirement that an animal for sacrifice must be healthy and unblemished.

B. THE GREEK GODS

I. THE DIVINITIES OF THE HEAVENS

1. Representatives of the Phenomena of the Thunderstorm

20. The most tremendous phenomenon in nature, and the first to attract the attention of mankind, is the thunderstorm. As this can be better compared to a violently raging battle than to any other event occurring on earth, it was first conceived of as a battle in which Zeus, the god of thunder and lightning, Athena, the goddess of lightning, the other Olympian gods that were friendly toward mankind, and the demigod, Hercules, are all arrayed against the monsters of the thunderstorm, the **Gigantes** ('Giants'). The latter, like the Cyclopes ('Cyclops'), are in the Odyssey imagined to be an earthly race of giants, living in the far west, hurling rocks for missiles, a race which is annihilated by the gods for its arrogance; but the later tradition, as in some other cases, seems to have preserved the earlier form. Accordingly in the art of the Hellenistic period, particularly, for example, on the frieze of the altar of Pergamum (now in the Berlin museum), they are represented with serpentine feet (lightning?). Originally Phlegra, the place of burning, was commonly mentioned as the battle ground; by which, probably, the glowing, illuminated sky is to be understood; later the scene of combat was removed to the peninsula (or the Attic deme) Pallene; finally, to Cumae, in Italy.

21. From a different point of view, however, the fall thunderstorms, breaking forth after the dry harvest time, were probably looked upon as a battle between the fructifying thunder god Zeus and his father, the sun god **Cronus**, who at the height of summer brought on the harvest and caused the luxuriant vegetation of spring to dry up. It is clear that Cronus was the sun god from his epithet, *Tītān;* and as in this contest other gods, according to the poets, were ranged beside Zeus as comrades for the fight, so there appeared on the side of Cronus, under the term Titānes ('Titans'), a series of names of beings of light, the meaning of which names, though appreciated in early worship, after a while largely faded away. With the help of the Cyclops ('round-eyed') Arges ('bright lightning'), Brontes ('thunder') and Steropes ('dazzling-eyed'), — whose single round eyes are the lightning, — they were vanquished and hurled down into Tartarus, the deepest part of the lower world.

22. To these conflicts of Zeus was added, later, that against **Typhōeus**, or Typhon ('the smoking, steaming one'). In him we have an embodiment (perhaps originating in Asia Minor) of the steam and smoke breaking from the earth in connection with earthquakes, and out of volcanoes, as well as of the mighty power working in those phenomena. Although he was armed with a hundred serpent heads darting forth fire, he, like the Titans, was cast down by Zeus into Tartarus. All this is a picture of the apparent conflict between the thunderstorm accompanying every volcanic eruption and those mighty forces of the depths which, at the end of the eruption, seem to sink back through the crater into the interior of the earth.

23. The victor in all these battles, the mighty god of the thunderstorm, a god, however, kindly disposed toward mankind, who sends down the fructifying rain, is **Zeus** (Lat. *Juppiter*). The stem of this name, which appears in the genitive Δι(ϝ)ός, goes back, like the Indian *Dyāus*, the German *Ziu*, and the Latin *Juppiter* (which is composed of *Diovis* or *Jovis* and *pater*), to the root *div* ('sky'); *i.e.* the name of the god of the thunderstorm is derived from the sky itself, of which the thunderstorm is a principal phenomenon. Corresponding to this idea, the chief attribute of Zeus, who is further characterized as the lightning god by the epithets *Keraunios* and *Kataibatēs*, is the lightning itself; and closely connected with this is the Aegis ('goatskin'), a representation of the thundercloud surrounded by serpentine lightning, which is usually pictured in later times as a shaggy skin with a border of serpents.

24. The victor in the battle of the storm came to be regarded as a powerful ruler of earthly combats (Zeus *Agētōr*, *Stratios*, *Areios*), who held victory (νίκη) in his hand; a conception which led Phidias to place the winged Nike on the outstretched hand of his statue of the Olympian Zeus. In his son Ares this side of Zeus's nature was developed into a god of war pure and simple. On account of the rain that falls during a thunderstorm, Zeus appears, on the other hand, as a rain dispenser bestowing fertility (*Hyetios*, *Ombrios*). In this capacity he begot from his sister Demeter, who is the female representative of the productive force of the cornfield, Persephone (Lat. *Prōserpina*), the subterranean protectress, and representative, of the seed corn. The same idea is expressed in the theogonic poetry by the relation of Uranus ('heaven') to Gaea ('earth'). In similar manner, according to an Argive legend, Zeus was united with Danaë under the guise of golden rain, and, according to a Theban legend, with Semele, who died in his embrace when, at her request, he approached her as he approaches Hera, *i.e.* as the god of the thunderstorm.

25. Zeus is also collector of the clouds (*Nephelēgeretēs*) and god of the winds (*Euanemos* and *Ūrios*). As such, however, he afterwards has associated with him Hermes, his son born of Maia (Pleias), the goddess of the rain cloud. To Zeus belong prodigies, birds of omen, and especially thunder and lightning themselves, and the eagle darting down upon its prey like a flash of lightning out of the clouds; and so he becomes a most important oracular god. The oak is sacred to him probably because it is an especially tall tree and is therefore frequently struck by lightning.

26. As thunderclouds settle about the mountain peaks, so Zeus as *Akraios* or *Koryphaios* makes his dwelling place upon them, his chief abodes being on Olympus on the borders of Thessaly and Macedonia, and on Lycaeus in Arcadia (which also is often called Olympus). On Mount Lycaeus human beings were offered to him. The legendary founder of this form of worship, Lycaon, was said to have slain here his own son, or grandson, and placed him before Zeus as a repast, *i.e.* offered him up. In punishment for this act he was changed into a wolf.

27. From his being the mightiest god the idea developed that Zeus was also the highest god (*Hypatos, Hypsistos*). From his mountain summit, like a king from his castle, he rules the surrounding country under the appellation of Zeus *Basileus*. As a symbol of his dominion he bears the scepter; he protects justice and all pious men, and punishes every wrong, especially perjury (Zeus *Horkios*), and any injury to a guest (Z. *Xenios*) or to one seeking protection (Z. *Hikesios*). It lies in his power to grant expiation of guilt, and purification (Z. *Katharsios*) (*cf.* Apollo). To him, therefore, as the protector of hearth and home (Z. *Herkeios*), the father of the family offered sacrifices; and to the same god, in his capacity of protector of the family (*Genethlios*), the head of the family sacrificed; and many ruling families claimed to derive their origin from him as their ancestor.

28. Side by side with the king of the gods stands their queen **Hērā**, who, like Juno, the goddess associated with Juppiter (the ruling lightning god of Italy), is probably to be regarded as the moon goddess and queen of the night. In Argos, where Hera was held in special honor, Hebe ('the bloom of youth') was considered the fruit of the union of this royal pair. Ares, also, the war god, and Hephaestus, the lightning god, are their children. As the masculine counterpart of Hebe appears Ganymedes (son of Tros or Laomedon), whom, on account of his beauty, Zeus caused to be kidnaped by an eagle, and to be made his cupbearer and favorite; for, like Ganymedes, Hebe too offers to the gods ambrosia and nectar; indeed she sometimes even bears the name Ganymeda.

29. Local traditions associated Zeus with numerous other goddesses and heroines representing the moon: at Dodona with Dione, a name which might, of course, in some old worship have belonged to Hera herself; at other places, with Selene, Europa, and Antiope. From the 'dark, beautiful-haired' Leto (Lat. *Lātōna*) he begot the sun god Apollo and the moon goddess Artemis; from Leda, whom he approached in the form of a swan, the moon heroine Helena ('Helen') and the hero of light Pollux. Again, Alcumena, whose origin was in the race of the Perseïdes ('shining ones'), became by him the mother of Hercules. But whether all these last-mentioned spouses may be regarded as moon heroines is doubtful.

30. The symbolizing poets have special regard to the moral side of the nature of Zeus, which afterwards came into prominence, when they designate Metis ('wisdom') and Themis ('law') as his wives, and represent him as begetting from the latter the Horae, Eunomia ('lawfulness'), Dike ('justice'), and Irene ('peace'), as well as the Moerae ('goddesses of fate'), who order human life. On similar grounds he figures as the father of the Graces and Muses. Finally, the legend of the birth and death of Zeus is based on a Cretan local worship. Here his father is the sun god Cronus, who devours his own children. But Cronus's spouse Rhea (a form of Ma, the mother of the gods, closely related to Cybele and Artemis, who were worshiped in Asia Minor), instead of giving him Zeus, hands him a stone, which was swallowed forthwith. Zeus, however, being suckled by the she-goat Amalthea (who represents the thundercloud, which dispenses nourishing moisture), grows rapidly in a cave of Mount Ida until he is in condition to overpower his father. (See § 21.)

31. In accordance with the conception prevailing in Homer, Phidias fashioned the artistically ideal figure of Zeus about 432 B.C. for the temple at Olympia, where the great national games were celebrated in his honor. The ancients believed that during the work there had been before the mind's eye of the artist the words of the Iliad (i. 528 *sq.*): —

> "He spoke, and awful bends his sable brows,
> Shakes his ambrosial curls, and gives the nod,
> The stamp of fate and sanction of the god:
> High heaven with trembling the dread signal took,
> And all Olympus to the centre shook."
>
> <div align="right">(<i>Pope's translation.</i>)</div>

But Lysippus (about 338 B.C.) is regarded as the creator of the most common type in the representations of Zeus in the art of later times, a type of which a noble example appears in the mask of Otricoli.

32. To a much smaller sphere than Zeus is his son, the lightning god **Hēphaestus** (Lat. *Volcānus*), confined, who probably was originally peculiar to a different Grecian tribe from that in which the worship of Zeus prevailed. He was born of Hera during a quarrel with Zeus (*i.e.* in a thunderstorm); but since he was lame (*i.e.* moved with a short, quick motion, like the lightning), his mother herself flung him down into the sea (a figurative expression for the descending lightning), where, in a cave, concealed for nine years, he was nursed by the sea goddesses Thetis and Eurynome. The latter part of this legend doubtless refers to that part of the year in which the lightning seems to be hidden away somewhere in the cloudy vault of the heavens. He is conducted back to heaven by Dionysus, *i.e.* in the spring; here he cleaves the head of Zeus by a stroke of his axe (lightning); amid loud cries of victory (thunder) the goddess of the thunderstorm, Pallas Athena, springs forth, — evidently a tale in which the phenomena occurring at the cleaving of a thundercloud by lightning have been attributed to the different divinities of the thunderstorm.

33. Out of regard to the fructifying power of the spring thunderstorms, Charis, the goddess of spring, is represented as being wedded to Hephaestus, according to the Iliad; in the Odyssey, however, he is the husband of Aphrodite, the goddess of love and fertility. After the invention of the art of working metal by the aid of fire, the phenomena of the thunderstorm were compared to the work in a forge, and so Hephaestus became the smith of the gods, with hammer, tongs, cap, and short working garment, who made weapons and ornaments for the immortals. Then when the Greeks became acquainted with the burning mountain on Lemnos and the volcanoes of Sicily and the Liparian islands, they transferred the forge of Hephaestus to these mountains, and called the Cyclops his comrades. The story now ran thus: because he had sided with his mother Hera in her quarrel with her husband, he was thrown down from Heaven upon the island Lemnos. This forthwith became one of the principal seats of his worship, a worship which blended with that of the oriental Cabiri ('great gods'), who were worshiped there and were in their nature related to him.

34. Another god of lightning and fire, originally, like Hephaestus, is **Promētheus** ('man of forethought'), who purloined fire from the gods, in order to give life, as well as fire, to the human beings that he had formed out of clay. Though he had previously been a friend of Zeus, he was now, in punishment for his deed, chained to a rock on Caucasus and tortured by an eagle which fed on his liver. It is Hephaestus who creates Pandora ('endowed by all'), the first woman, through whom, according to the familiar story of Pandora's box, all evils come upon the race of men created by Prometheus.

35. With these gods of the thunderstorm, who are principally the embodiments of the lightning flash, are intimately associated a series of female divinities of the thunderstorm, in whom the appearance of the thundercloud comes into special prominence. Everywhere in Greece and in her colonies, but most of all in Athens, which was named for her, **Athēnā** (Lat. *Minerva*) was worshiped as the goddess that sends down lightning, rain, dew, and mist. She is designated as a goddess of the lightning by her epithet *Pallas*, 'the brandisher' of lightning, which is conceived of as a spear; therefore in early times her statues, representing her with poised spear, were called *Palladia*. Like her father Zeus, she wears the Aegis, and with it the Gorgon's head (*Gorgoneion*), which, according to the Argive myth, she received from Perseus, but, according to the Attic myth, won for herself in single combat.

36. The three **Gorgones** ('Gorgons'), who live in the far west, — especially one of them, the mortal Medusa, — are properly female representatives of the thunderclouds; but, like the Giants and the Cyclops, they embody only the terrible side of the phenomenon. Their vesture is as black as the thundercloud; their fiery glance turns to stone, as the lightning's stroke stuns or kills; their bellowing is the roar of the thunder; wings carry them through the air. When the head of Medusa was cut off, the monster Chrysaor ('gold-sword,' the golden flash of the lightning) sprang from her body, and also the winged horse Pegasus (the thundercloud), at the stamp of whose hoof (lightning) the spring of the Muses, Hippocrene ('horse spring'), which inspires all poets, gushed forth on Mount Helicon. After serving Bellerophon, Pegasus bears in heaven the lightning of Zeus. Medusa was killed by Athena for the same reason as that for which the Giants were conquered by Zeus. That is, in the phenomena of the thunderstorm the element of power that is hostile to mankind, embodied in these monsters, soon disappears; but rain and fertility, which men regard as gifts of the divinity of the storm, endure after the storm has vented its rage. Like Zeus, Athena becomes, on account of this contest and victory, the goddess of war and victory in general, so that she bears the epithets *Promachos* ('leader of the combat') and *Nīkē* ('victory').

37. In the dry season of the year, the rain, which promotes the growth of vegetation, sometimes pours from the thundercloud; and so Athena was the protectress of the chief sources of the wealth of Attica, namely, fruit culture and agriculture, and consequently of the cultivated land. Therefore the second principal type of her representation in art exhibits a matronly, enthroned goddess, who is usually called Athena *Polias* ('goddess of the city'). On the Acropolis of Athens was an ancient olive tree, which, it was said, the goddess had caused to spring up when she strove with Poseidon for the dominion over the country.

38. To agriculture especially is to be referred the myth of the serpent-formed **Erichthonius**, or **Erechtheus**. These two names at Athens stood originally for the same person, and really represented the seed corn growing up out of the lap of the earth (their mother Gaea), under the protection of Athena, the goddess of the thunderstorm, and her maidservants, the dew sisters Aglauros ('the one living in the open air'), Herse ('dew'), and Pandrosos ('dew'). The father of both Erichthonius and Erechtheus is Hephaestus, the god of the thunderstorm, who during the spring storms cleaves the hard crust of the earth and fertilizes it. It was supposed to be in his honor and that of Athena that the very ancient *Chalkeia* ('forge festival') had been instituted, at which the invention of the plow and the birth of Erechtheus were celebrated. Erichthonius and Erechtheus came at length to be distinguished. The latter was considered a national god living in a cave on the Acropolis, and, still later, as a king of Athens. The dew sisters now appear under various names as his daughters. In the Erechtheum he was worshiped as a hero in the form of a serpent, in connection with the worship of Athena and Poseidon. As the protecting goddess of agriculture Athena was honored also by sacred plowings at the foot of the Acropolis in the beginning of seedtime, and especially at the old harvest festival of the *Panathēnaia* from the 24th to the 29th of Hecatombaion (beginning of August), a festival which from the time of Pisistratus was observed every fifth year with special splendor. A torch race, prize contests for musicians and dancers, and races between ships of war were arranged for these occasions. The chief day of the festival was the 28th, the birthday of the goddess, on which they brought her a new robe (Peplus), embroidered by the ladies of the highest rank in Athens. During the festal procession through the city this was fastened like a sail to a chariot made to imitate the form of a ship. Priests, old men, women and maidens, and the whole body of men capable of bearing arms, marched along with it, amid a display of the greatest magnificence, up the Acropolis to the ancient temple of the goddess. The splendid reliefs on the frieze of the cella of the Parthenon still serve to bring this festal procession before our eyes.

39. This Peplus, moreover, calls attention to another very significant side of the nature of the goddess. The thundercloud, in which the lightnings rush hither and thither, and similarly the mist, which often covers everything as with a veil, were conceived of as a delicately woven fabric; and so the goddess with whom these phenomena were associated, under the name Athena *Erganē* ('worker'), came to be considered the inventress of the arts of spinning and weaving. As such she transformed into a spider the skillful Lydian weaver Arachne ('spider'), who dared to engage with her in a trial of skill. After she had once become the inventress of an art in which skill is of great importance for the ordinary relations of life, many other similar inventions were ascribed to her. So she developed gradually into the goddess of wisdom in general, and in that connection into the protectress of learning; and, in Hesiod, Metis ('wisdom') appears as her mother. Of course it may be that some additional influence to emphasize this phase of her character was exerted by the idea of her clear shining glance (suggested in her epithet γλαυκῶπις, and in the fact that the owl is her sacred bird), which in human beings indicates a spiritual life, and which properly belongs to Athena on account of the same characteristic in the lightning. Also a further explanation may be sought in the notion of the fiery essence of the soul itself; for it was on this ground that the formation and animation of the human race were ascribed to Prometheus, god of lightning, and to Hephaestus, god of fire.

40. Athena's ideal figure in art was made by Phidias, who likewise has been generally credited with having created the type of the so-called Athena *Promachos* in a colossal bronze statue placed upon the Acropolis under the open sky. It was the same sculptor who fashioned in gold and ivory for the Parthenon the Athena *Parthenos* ('maiden'), holding on her right hand Nike ('victory'). She appears always serious, even austere, but full of composure, and with an expression of high intellectuality; she always wears a long robe, and is often distinguished by the Aegis worn over this.

41. The **Erinyes** ('the angry ones'), black, winged, stalking swiftly along in the dark clouds, are, like the Gorgons described above, the embodiments of the grim thunderclouds which threaten destruction. Their glance of flame and their fiery breath, like the serpents twining about their heads, represent the darting lightning. The same idea is signified by the torch and the whip which they brandish, the latter of which produces a state of madness and stupefaction in whomsoever they strike. But since the clouds on the horizon seem to rise up out of the earth, imagination removed the abode of the Erinyes to the lower world; thus from being black divinities of the thunderstorm, who bring death, they became goddesses of death and vengeance. Their wild raging was conceived of as a pursuit or a hunt, so that they were themselves compared to hounds. On being transferred to the realm of morals they became pursuers of those that had committed heinous crimes, especially of those who, transgressing the laws of family rights, had injured a parent or elder brother; on the other hand they protect the stranger and the sacredness of an oath. But by offerings and prayers, even the 'angry ones' can be conciliated, and so they were worshiped in Sicyon and Argos as *Eumenides* ('well-disposed'), in Athens as *Semnai* ('the honored').

42. Near the Gorgons dwell their sisters and guardians, the **Graeae** ('old women'), Pephredo, Enyo, and Deino ('the terrible'). They are probably representatives of the gray clouds preceding the thunderstorm proper, in which the lightning harmlessly darts from one cloud to another (heat lightning). Therefore they appear as old women, who possess only one eye and only one tooth between them (in both these figures representing the lightning), who surrender these to each other, however, for various purposes.

Gigantes: Hesiod, Theog. 185; Ovid. Met. i. 152 *sq.*
Cronus (Saturn): Homer, Il. *passim;* Hesiod, Theog. 137; Ovid, Met. i. 113 *sq.*, Amor. iii. 8, 35; Vergil, Aen. vii. 180, viii. 319, 357; Keats, Hyperion i. 249: —

>Shall scare that infant thunderer, rebel Jove,
>And bid old Saturn take his throne again.

Milton, Par. L. i. 510: —

>Titan, heaven's firstborn,
>With his enormous brood, and birthright seized

> By younger Saturn; he from mightier Jove
> (His own and Rhea's son) like measure found;
> So Jove usurping reign'd.

Chaucer, Knight's Tale 470, *et passim*.
    Titan as sun god: Shak., Venus and Adonis 30: —
> And Titan, tired in the mid-day heat.

Spenser, F. Q. i. iv. 8, xi. 33.
    Titanes: Hesiod, Theog. 207; Hyginus, *Pref.*
    Cyclopes: Homer, Odys. vi. 5, viii., ix. *passim;* Hesiod, Theog. 139; Euripides, Cyclops; Vergil, Geor. i. 471: —
> Quotiens Cyclopum effervere in agros
> Vidimus undantem ruptis fornacibus Aetnam,
> Flammarumque globos liquefactaque volvere saxa!

Aen. iii. 569, xi. 263, Geor. iv. 170 *sq.;* Ovid, Met. xiii. 744 *sq.*, xiv. 167 *sq.;* Pope, Thebais i. 306: —
> Th' o'erlabour'd Cyclop from his task retires.

Shak., Titus Andronicus iv. 3, 46, Hamlet ii. 2, 511.
    Typhoeus: Hesiod, Theog. 821; Ovid, Met. v. 325 *sq.;* Spenser, F. Q. i. v. 35.
    Zeus (Juppiter): The noun stem DIV, DYU, became early a deification. The all-comprehending heavenly spaces suggest the divine presence. The word PITR ('father') was often joined to this stem. In the following hymns DYĀUS PITĀ ('sky-father') was worshiped among the ancient Hindus. The references are to all the places in the Rig Veda where the epithet PITR is added: Rig Veda i. 71. 5, i. 89. 4, i. 90. 7, i. 164. 33, i. 191. 6, iv. 1. 10, v. 43. 2, vi. 51. 5. In Hindu mythology, however, Indra corresponds in attributes to the Greek Zeus and Roman Juppiter more than any other god in the Indian Pantheon. The following verses from Rig Veda i., describing him as the whirler of the thunderbolt, are representative of many such ascriptions to his might which abound in the Veda. Indra, Rig Veda i. 32: —

1. The heroic deeds of Indra I shall declare which foremost he having the thunderbolt has accomplished. | He smote the dragon, he bored after the waters, he cut in sunder the bellies of the (cloud) mountains.

2. He smote the dragon lying on the mountains. Tvastar forged for him the whizzing thunderbolt. | As lowing kine, flowing suddenly the water ran down to the confluence.

3. With the lust of a bull he took the Soma, he drank of the extract in the vessels. |

The generous Indra took the missile, the destructive thunderbolt, he smote the firstborn of dragons.

15. Indra is king of him who goes, of him who rests, and of the tame, of the horned beast, (Indra) possessing the thunderbolt on his arm. | That king rules the busy folk. He has surrounded them as a felly the spokes.

Hesiod, Theog. 72; Homer, Il. i. *passim*, xiv. 203: —

ὅτε τε Κρόνον εὐρύοπα Ζεὺς
γαίης νέρθε καθεῖσε καὶ ἀτρυγέτοιο θαλάσσης.

Ovid, Met. i. 113, Ars Amat. i. 635; Vergil, Aen. vii. 219; Hyginus, Fab. clv.; (As the Sky, Horace, Od. i. 22, 20, iii. 10, 8;) Pope, Thebais i. 357: —

When Jove descended in almighty gold;

Rape of the Lock v. 49: —

Jove's thunder roars, heaven trembles all around.

Shak., Cymbeline v. 4, 32: —

With Mars fall out, with Juno chide;

The Tempest v. 1, 45, Measure for Measure ii. 2, 111, Hamlet iii. 4, 56; Spenser, F. Q. i. i. 6, iv. 11; Chaucer, Knight's Tale 2177, *et passim*.

Uranus: Varuṇa (root VR = 'cover') was an early deification of the expanse. A hymn in the Atharva Veda praises the god as the all-knowing divine presence. The stars which studded the heavens at night became, in the poetic imagination, the thousand eyes of Varuṇa looking down upon the world. A portion of the hymn is translated here. Atharva Veda iv. 16: —

1. The great one, lord of these worlds, sees, as if close at hand. | Whoever thinks he is acting stealthily, the gods know it all.

2. Whoever stands, and goes, and whoever stoops, whoever hides, whoever withdraws, | Whatever two (persons) sitting together devise, Varuṇa the king knows it (for he is there) as a third.

3. The earth is of Varuṇa the king and yonder heaven, great, possessing distant ends. | And the two oceans are Varuṇa's stomach and in this little water he is hidden.

4. Who would go far beyond heaven will not escape from Varuṇa the king. | His spies from heaven traverse the world. Thousand-eyed they look upon the earth.

5. All this Varuṇa the king knows, what is between heaven and earth (and) what is beyond. |

Numbered by him are the winkings of men's eyes. As a gamester knows his dice, he takes note of them.

Lycaon: Ovid, Met. i. 198 *sq*.

Hera (Juno): Homer, Il. i. *passim;* Hesiod, Theog. 454; Ovid, Ars Amat. i. 635, Met. iii. *passim;* Vergil, Aen. i. *passim;* Hyginus, Fab. xiii.; Milton, Par. L. ix. 18:—

> Or Neptune's ire or Juno's, that so long
> Perplex'd the Greek and Cytherea's son.

Shak., The Tempest iv. 1, 131, Antony and Cleopatra iv. 15, 34; Spenser, F. Q. i. iv. 17.

Hebe: Homer, Il. v. 722, Od. xi. 603; Hesiod, Theog. 922; Ovid, Met. ix. 400; Milton, Comus 290:—

> As smooth as Hebe's their unrazor'd lips;

L'Allegro 29.

Ganymedes: Ovid, Met. x. 155:—

> Rex superum Phrygii quondam Ganymedis amore
> Arsit;

xi. 756; Vergil, Aen. i. 28.

Dione: Homer, Il. v. 381:—

$$\Delta\iota\omega\nu\eta, \delta\hat{\iota}\alpha\ \theta\epsilon\acute{a}\omega\nu.$$

Ovid, Ars Amat. iii. 3, Amor. i. 14, 33.

Rhea: Hesiod, Theog. 453; Ovid, Fast. iv. 201.

Hephaestus (Vulcan): Hesiod, Theog. 927; Homer, Il. i. 590:—

> ἤδη γάρ με καὶ ἄλλοτ' ἀλεξέμεναι μεμαῶτα
> ῥῖψε ποδὸς τεταγὼν ἀπὸ βηλοῦ θεσπεσίοιο,
> πᾶν δ' ἦμαρ φερόμην, ἅμα δ' ἠελίῳ καταδύντι
> κάππεσον ἐν Λήμνῳ, ὀλίγος δ' ἔτι θυμὸς ἐνῆεν.

Ovid, Ars Amat. ii. 741; Vergil, Aen. viii. 370 *sq.;* Milton, Par. L. i. 740:—

> And how he fell
> From Heaven, they fabled, thrown by angry Jove
> Sheer o'er the crystal battlements; from morn
> To noon he fell, from noon to dewy eve,
> A summer's day; and with the setting sun
> Dropped from the zenith like a falling star,
> On Lemnos the Ægean isle.

Cowper, Translation from Milton vii:—

> When Jove had hurled him to the Lemnian coast
> So Vulcan sorrowed for Olympus lost.

Shak., Much Ado about Nothing i. 1, 187; Chaucer, Knight's Tale 1364.

Prometheus: Hesiod, Theog. 510; Aeschylus, Prometheus Vinctus; Vergil, Ecl. vi. 42; Hyginus, Fab. cxliv.; Cowper, Translation from Milton, Epigram on the Inventor of Guns: —

> Praise in old time the sage Prometheus won,
> Who stole ethereal radiance from the sun;
> But greater he whose bold invention strove
> To emulate the fiery bolts of Jove.

Translation from Milton, To his Father: —

> Man's heavenly source, and which retaining still
> Some scintillations of Promethean fire,
> Bespeaks him animated from above.

Shak., Love's Labour's Lost iv. 3, 304, Othello v. 2, 12, Titus Andronicus ii. 1, 17.

Pandora: Hyginus, Fab. cxlii.; Milton, Par. L. iv. 714: —

> More lovely than Pandora, whom the gods
> Endow'd with all their gifts.

Pallas Athena (Minerva): Hesiod, Theog. 923: —

> Αὐτὸς δ' ἐκ κεφαλῆς γλαυκώπιδα γείνατ' Ἀθήνην.

Homer, Il. ii. 157, i. *passim*; Ovid, Fast. iii. 5: —

> Ipse vides manibus peragi fera bella Minervae:
> Num minus ingenuis artibus illa vacat?

Ars Amat. i. 625, 745; Vergil, Aen. v. 704, ii. *passim*; Horace, Ars Poet. 385: —

> Tu nihil invita dices faciesve Minerva.

Pope, The Dunciad i. 10: —

> Ere Pallas issued from the Thund'rer's head.

Gorgones: Ovid, Met. iv. 618; Vergil, Aen. vi. 289; Milton, Comus 447: —

> What was that snaky-headed Gorgon shield
> That wise Minerva wore, unconquer'd virgin,
> Wherewith she freez'd her foes to congeal'd stone?

Browning, Protus 4: —

> Loric and low-browed Gorgon on the breast.

Erechtheus: Vergil, Geor. iii. 113; Hyginus, Fab. clxvi.
Arachne: Ovid, Met. vi. 5 *sq.*
Graeae: Hesiod, Theog. 270.

D

Erinyes (Eumenides): Hesiod, Theog. 185; Aeschylus, Eumenides; Ovid, Met. i. 241, iv. 490, xi. 14; Vergil, Aen. ii. 337, 573, iv. 469, vii. 447; Pope, Ode on St. Cecilia's Day 69: —
>The Furies sink upon their iron beds
>And snakes uncurl'd hang list'ning round their heads.

Spenser, F. Q. i. iii. 36, v. 31.

2. Divinities of the Wind

43. As the wind itself shares one of its principal characteristics, swiftness, with the thunderclouds, so the divinities to whose activity was traced the power manifesting itself in the wind resembled the representatives of the thundercloud in many ways. A middle ground between the two seems to have been occupied by the **Harpȳiae** ('the swift robbers'), Aëllo ('storm-swift'), and Ocypete ('swift-flying'), whose field of action was in the storm clouds. They are represented as winged and with a horse's shape, also as creatures with the head and bust of a woman, and the body of a bird, figures which were intended to suggest their swiftness. They came to be regarded as goddesses of death, swiftly snatching away their victims; evidently because it was supposed that souls, being like air or smoke, were, on leaving the body, carried away by the storm.

44. Closely allied to the Harpies are the **wind gods** proper, who often, as enemies or as lovers, pursue them; for in the earliest times the wind gods too were believed to have the form of a horse, later that of bearded men, taking long strides, with wings on their shoulders and often also on their feet. Sometimes they have faces looking both ways, forwards and backwards, a conception which probably has reference to the changeableness in the direction of the wind. There were distinguished in the earlier times only Boreas (north), Zephyrus (west), Notus (south), and, somewhat later, Eurus (east), who were considered the sons of Astraeus ('starry vault of heaven') and Eos ('dawn'). Like the Harpies, they are of a rapacious nature. Boreas, in particular, kidnaped the beautiful Orithyia, the daughter of Erechtheus, from the bank of the Ilissus, — a story which perhaps typifies the morning mist being carried off by the wind. The ruler of the winds is Aeolus ('the shifting one'), who dwells on a floating island in the far west, and keeps them confined in a cave.

45. According to the most probable interpretation **Hermēs** (Lat. *Mercurius*), too, was originally a wind god; but with him, as in the case of Apollo, the relation to his native element was almost entirely obscured by that side of his nature which is concerned purely with human life and customs. So his fundamental signification can be determined only by the agreement of many of his functions with the attributes of the wind and with those of divinities that can be clearly shown to be wind gods. He was the messenger of Zeus, because the wind seems to come from heaven; and for the same reason he came to be considered the son of the god of the heavens and of Maia, the goddess of the rain clouds, and was said to have been born on Olympus, or in the cave Cyllene (*i.e.* the cave of the clouds). As messenger he carried the herald's staff (κηρύκειον, Lat. *cādūceus*), which had originally the form of a walking stick, or shepherd's staff, but was later usually like a forked branch twisted.

46. On account of the swiftness and power of the wind Hermes became the god of bodily exercise (H. *Agōnios*), worshiped in race courses and wrestling-schools. In harmony with the idea that he was god of the wind, he was equipped with wings, which he is usually represented as wearing on his shoes or feet, and on his traveling-hat (Petasos) or head, but not, at least in the classical period, on his shoulders. Because the wind whistles, Hermes is said to have invented the flute and syrinx, and also, by an easy process of reasoning, the lyre. And because the wind, without any apparent reason, arbitrarily changes, Hermes is the god of changing, unstable, fortune and chance, so that his herald's staff assumes the significance of a magic wand, which similarly among the ancient Germans was an attribute of the wind god Wodan. But as the traveler is dependent on the favor of wind and weather, and in a foreign land can always get his bearings by noticing the direction of the prevailing wind, so Hermes is the protector and guide of the wanderer. Sacred to him were the heaps of stones or the stone columns that served as waymarks, which were often adorned with a head of Hermes and called Hermae.

47. The wind gods are robbers; and so Hermes too was looked upon as the one who drives away herds of cattle (clouds), and hence as god of thieves and deceivers. Boreas kidnaps a beautiful maiden; Hermes plays the impetuous lover with the nymphs. It was also in connection with this idea that he was regarded as the promoter of all sorts of rural fertility in animals and plants. Yet the fact that this attribute of his is brought forward prominently would appear striking, if he were not also, as the son of the rain goddess Maia, properly to be regarded as the rain bringer, dispensing fertility. In ancient times a manifold fructifying effect was really attributed to the wind. On this ground Hermes was regarded as god of shepherds (*Nomios*) and bestower of an abundance of flocks and herds (*Epimēlios*) and, at the same time, of prosperity in general, an idea which again is connected with his significance as a god of fortune. It was because of this latter attribute that he was supposed to promote and foster money-making on land and sea. So merchants, whom he protected on their journeys, spread his worship everywhere, and especially carried it to Rome, where as Mercurius ('god of merchandise') he was held in the highest esteem.

48. As the Harpies were considered goddesses of death, carrying off human beings, so Hermes *Psȳchopompos* ('soul-conductor') guided into the lower world the souls ($\psi v \chi \acute{\eta}$ = 'breath') of the dead, which were conceived of as airy, or sometimes as like birds or bats. He was also thought to send visions, which are intimately associated with souls, and so became god of death and of sleep.

As god of shepherds Hermes was worshiped in the country, particularly in Arcadia; as god of commerce, in Athens and other commercial cities. In the former conception he carries, besides the above-mentioned symbols, a ram; in the latter, especially in the imperial epoch, a purse. In the older art he is usually represented as a mature man with pointed beard, but in works of Ionic origin is often even then conceived of as a youth. Later this is his regular form; he is then clothed with only a chlamys, or is almost entirely nude, as he appears in the splendid statue by Praxiteles found at Olympia. The child upon his arm is the young Dionysus, whom he is carrying to the nymphs to be nursed. (*Cf.* § 90.)

Harpyiae: Hesiod, Theog. 267; Vergil, Aen. iii. 212, 245; Hyginus, Fab. xix.; Pope, Im. of Horace Sat. ii. 25: —
> Oldfield with more than Harpy throat endued.

Boreas: Hesiod, Theog. 379; Ovid, Trist. iii. 10. 14, 11. 8; Vergil, Geor. i. 93, 370, Aen. xii. 365; Shak., Troilus and Cressida i. 3, 37.

Zephyrus: Homer, Il. ii. 147; Ovid, Her. xiv. 39: —
> Ut leni Zephyro graciles vibrantur aristae,
> Frigida populeas ut quatit aura comas.

Vergil, Geor. i. 371; Pope, Essay on Criticism 366: —
> Soft is the strain when Zephyr gently blows.

Chaucer, Prologue 5.

Aeolus: Homer, Od. x. 1 *sq.*; Vergil, Aen. i. 50–101; Horace, Od. iii. 30, 13; Pope, The Rape of the Lock iv. 81: —
> A wondrous bag with both her hands she binds,
> Like that where once Ulysses held the winds;

Thebais i. 488: —
> At once the rushing winds with roaring sound
> Burst from th' Aeolian caves, and rend the ground.

Shak., King Henry VI. pt. ii. iii. 2, 92.

Hermes (Mercury): Homer, Il. i. *passim*, Od. i. *passim*; Hesiod, Theog. 938; Ovid, Fast. v. 673 *sq.*; Vergil, Aen. iv. 222 *sq.*, 558; Hyginus, Fab. clx., cci.; Milton, Par. L. xi. 132: —
> Charmed with Arcadian pipe, the pastoral reed
> Of Hermes, or his opiate rod.

Shak., Love's Labour's Lost v. 2, 940: —
> The words of Mercury are harsh after the songs of Apollo;

King Richard III. ii. 1, 88, Hamlet iii. 4, 58, Antony and Cleopatra iv. 15, 36, Troilus and Cressida ii. 2, 45; Chaucer, Knight's Tale 527.

3. Divinities of Light

49. Among the divinities of the sky belong the representatives of the sun, the moon, the stars, and other phenomena of light. **Apollō** was probably a **sun god**, whose worship was very common among the Dorians and Ionians, though in historic times he stood for the god of all that is beautiful and good, and was likewise the chief representative of good morals and civil order. Aside from his epithets, *Lycius* ('bright'), *Phoebus* ('shining'), *Chrȳsocomās* ('golden-haired'), and *Epopsios* ('overseeing'), and his worship as guide of the wanderer, and protector of navigation (A. *Agyieus*, and *Delphīnios*; *cf.* § 75), his original significance is indicated, first, by the circumstance that all his festivals occurred in the warm season. On the 7th day of Thargelion (May-June) his birthday was celebrated, especially in Delos; for, pursued by the hate of the jealous Hera, his mother Leto, after long wandering, finally found a refuge upon this rocky island, which up to that time had been itself without a fixed abode, driven about over the waves; and there she bore the twins, Apollo and Artemis. In some localities, particularly at Delphi, the next most important place of the worship of Apollo, there was celebrated at about the same time the festival of his return from the land of the Hyperboreï, a mythical realm of eternal light and blessed peace, which in later times was supposed to be in the far north; while in other places it was believed that Apollo spent the winter months in Ethiopia or Lycia, *i.e.* in the southern land of light.

50. Immediately after his birth he is threatened by the hostile powers of winter and darkness; yet the young god victoriously subdues them. This is the significance of the story of his killing the dragon Python or Delphyne, the victory which was celebrated by the festival of the Pythian games. Since the growth of vegetation in the pastures and cultivated fields depends upon the sun, Apollo becomes the god of pastures (*Nomios*) and protector of cattle breeding; therefore in Sparta and

elsewhere the festival of *Karneia* ('feast of the ram') was celebrated in his honor; and Aristaeus ('the best god'), the representative of agriculture, cattle raising, and bee culture, was called his son. For the same reason harvest festivals were celebrated in his honor: in Delos, the *Dēlia;* in Sparta, the *Hyakinthia;* in Athens, the *Thargēlia* and *Pyanepsia*. At the Spartan festival the vegetation, ripened and killed by the beams of the sun, was represented under the form of Hyacinthus, the personified spring flower, and the legend was that Apollo, at play, had inadvertently killed this favorite of his by a throw of the discus, but had then caused the flower to spring forth out of his blood as it flowed to the ground.

51. Usually, however, the rays of the sun are regarded as arrows; therefore Apollo carries as his weapons arrows and a silver bow. The 'far-shooter' (*Hekatos, Hekaergos, Hekatēbolos*) comes to be considered an aid in battle (*Boēdromios*); but, on the other hand, since in the south the heat of the midsummer sun produces the much-dreaded pestilence and other sicknesses, he becomes the god of the plague. To propitiate him, feasts of atonement must be celebrated, and so at the *Thargēlia* in Athens even human beings are said to have been offered as vicarious sacrifices, that he might pardon the rest. Yet, as he sends sickness, so he can ward it off; therefore he is invoked as the defender from evil (*Alexikakos*), savior (*Sōtēr*), and healing physician (*Paiēōn, Ūlios*); and the physician of the gods, Aesculapius, is considered his son. These characteristics, together with his general nature as a god of light, by being transferred from the realm of the physical to that of the spiritual, cause him to appear as a redeemer from all guilt and the chief representative of purification and expiation (Λ. *Kathársios*). In this capacity his attribute is the laurel branch (δάφνη) with which one needing pardon is dismissed; but the symbol of the wolf, which has been interpreted as an emblem of the fugitive murderer, is probably only the result of a confusion between the words λύκος ('wolf') and Λύκειος ('the bright one').

52. In later times all other phases of Apollo's nature were subordinate to his special character as **god of oracles**. The most important place of prophecy in all Greece was his oracle at Delphi, which is mentioned as early as the Iliad; but he gave oracular responses also at Didymoi near Miletus, Claros near Colophon, and Abai in Phocis. At these places a priestess, who by drinking from a sacred spring had brought herself into an inspired state, uttered significant words, which were then interpreted by a priest standing beside her, and thus became a response. At Delphi the priestess, who was called Pythia ('the understanding one,' *cf.* ἐπυθόμην), sat on a tripod over a fissure in the ground while giving the oracle. Furthermore, since the oracular responses of Apollo were usually composed in verse, Apollo was considered the protector and friend of poetry, song, and its customary accompaniment, namely, playing on the lyre. So he became leader of the Muses, and received as an additional emblem the lyre invented by Hermes.

53. In art Apollo is represented by the ideal form of a perfectly-developed, slender youth, beardless, except in archaic art, and with long hair falling in ringlets. Usually he is nude, or with only a little cloak (*chlamys*) thrown over his shoulder or his left arm. As his distinguishing symbols he carries a bow and arrows. A variety of this type, Apollo at rest, with his arm resting on his head, seems to have originated with Praxiteles. As leader of the Muses he is represented with a long, Ionian garment (*chitōn*), a lyre, and a laurel wreath,— a conception which, at least in the more animated form of its representation, is believed to have been furnished by Scopas.

54. As the ethical side of Apollo's nature was more fully developed, by degrees his significance in the visible world was forgotten, and the active force typified in the sun god was transferred to **Helios**, who was probably from a very early period regarded by the inhabitants of the island of Rhodes as their chief god. For, while his worship in the rest of Greece was relatively insignificant, there he was so highly honored that a brilliant festival, the *Hēlieia*, was celebrated for him. At the same place was erected in his honor, about 280 B.C., at the entrance of the harbor, the celebrated bronze statue (made by Chares of Lindos) known as the Colossus of Rhodes. On account of the apparent movement of the sun it was believed that Helios rode along in the heavens in a glittering chariot, drawn by four swift horses. He himself was pictured to the imagination as in the bloom of young manhood, with a sparkling crown upon his head, which was covered with long curling locks. From the sea goddess Clymene he begot Phaëthon ('the shining'), who perished in an attempt to manage the chariot of the sun for a day in his father's place. On the island of Thrinacia were said to be pastured the milk-white herds of cattle and flocks of sheep belonging to Helios, by which are probably to be understood the bright little clouds which with us also are frequently described as "fleecy," and among the Germans are called *Schäfchen* ('lambkins'). The heliotrope, which always turns toward the sun, was believed to be his beloved Clytia metamorphosed into a flower.

55. The **moon** among the Greeks and Romans was given a feminine name (σελήνη, *lūna*); and the power which people believed they saw exerted by it was ascribed to goddesses, who in different tribes bore various names. During nights when the moon shines bright the dew falls more abundantly than at other times; therefore the moon goddesses were regarded as dispensers of dew, and as protectresses of the growth of plants, as well as of the abundance of game depending on vegetation for food. The relation to human fertility which is prominent in all these goddesses is probably based upon the influence that the moon appears to exercise upon the life of women.

56. The latter characteristic comes into the foreground in the case of **Hērā** (Lat. *Jūnō*), who was worshiped throughout Greece, but especially in Argos. She is the protectress of wedlock (H. *Zygiā, Teleiā*), and the jealous representative of lawful wives and their rights. The goddess of birth, Ilithyia, was considered to be her daughter. The festivals in honor of Hera always came on the day of the new moon, and likewise the celebrations of her marriage with Zeus (ἱερὸς γάμος), at Argos in the spring, at Athens in the month of weddings, Gamelion (January–February). Being spouse and sister of Zeus, she was the queen of the gods, and as such Polyclitus represented her (about 420 b.c.) in his statue of gold and ivory made for her restored temple, which was situated between Argos and Mycenae. There she sat upon a throne, fully clothed, a crown upon her head, in her right hand a pomegranate, which on account of its many seeds was an emblem of fruitfulness. In her left hand she held the royal scepter, with a cuckoo, the messenger of spring, as its crown. Similarly it is as a queen that she appears before us in the excellent colossal bust of the Villa Ludovisi, a work which may belong to about the middle of the fourth century B.C.

57. To **Artemis** (Lat. *Diāna*), daughter of Zeus and Leto, and twin sister of Apollo, was attributed particularly, besides her influence upon childbirth (A. *Īlīthyia*), another one of the various functions of moon goddesses, namely, a fostering care over the abundant game in field and forest. She then developed into the goddess of hunting (*Agrōteira*), probably because, being a light-goddess, she is, like her brother Apollo, armed with bow and arrows; moreover, the swift motion of the moon through the so-called Zodiac reminds one of a hunt. At Athens the festival of *Elaphēbolia* ('stag hunt') was celebrated in her honor, and the hind is represented as her constant companion. As a chaste and austere maiden she punished with great severity every violation of chastity. The hunter Actaeon, son of Aristaeus, who had accidentally surprised her and her attendant nymphs bathing, was changed by her into a stag, that his own dogs might tear him to pieces; and on similar grounds she killed the giant hunter Orion, who was then transferred as a constellation to the sky.

58. The many-breasted goddess of Ephesus, conceived of as the nourisher of all life, was so similar to the protectress of the beasts of the forest and field that she also was called Artemis; yet she seems to have been originally, like Rhea and Cybele, only a local, modified type of the great maternal goddess of nature and war, Ma or Ammas ('mother'), who was worshiped by the Indo-European inhabitants of Asia Minor. To the nymphs attending Artemis as huntresses correspond the Amazones ('Amazons') in the service of this Asiatic goddess. Evidently they were originally like her, and lived, according to the ancient myth, on the southern coast of the Black Sea, *i.e.* on the Thermodon and Iris in Pontus, while the chief abode of Ma herself was in that very region, at Comana on the Iris. The Amazons fought as bold riders against Bellerophon, Hercules, Theseus, and Achilles. Accordingly they are represented in art mostly as powerful, beautiful riders, with short garments and semicircular (or Boeotian) shields, and are frequently armed with the battle-axe. Phidias and Polyclitus made also statues representing in each case an Amazon fatigued by the exertions of battle.

59. In Athens, Delos, and Epidaurus, Artemis bore the epithet ἑκάτη ('the far-shooter'). So it is clear that the goddess **Hecatē**, — daughter of the Titan Perses ('the shining one') and Asteria ('naiad of the stars'), — although her worship developed quite independently, was by nature very closely related to Artemis. Hecate was worshiped principally in Caria and the adjacent provinces of Asia Minor, where she seems to have been an ancient goddess of the country. In Greece proper she was really worshiped only on the east coast, where she was particularly honored on the island of Aegina by secret rites or mysteries (*Mystēria*). In earlier times she was represented with but one body, fully clothed, in her hands two burning torches, which were attributed to her because of her character as a goddess of light; but Alcamenes (toward the end of the fifth century B.C.) made for the Acropolis at Athens a figure representing her as having three bodies (τριπρόσωπος, *triformis*). These three bodies were placed back to back so that one of them constantly, like the crescent moon, looked towards the left, another, like the waning moon, towards the right, while the one standing between them, like the full moon, turned her face towards the beholder. The dish and measure that she carries in representations of this type characterize her as dispenser of dew. Afterwards her worship at the crossroads was associated with these figures, and hence she was called *Trioditis*, Lat. *Trivia* ('the goddess of the crossroads').

60. Hecate was a kind of patron goddess of the belief in ghosts and witchcraft, and, as a natural consequence, a goddess of the lower world. The first of these functions belongs properly to the moon goddess as the mistress of the dismal nighttime; but she came to be considered a witch because she herself, *i.e.* the moon, has the power of changing her own form, a trick that plays an important part in all witchcraft. Therefore she was regarded as the mother of the enchantresses Circe and Medea ('the shrewd,' 'the cunning woman'). Her association with the realm of the dead, however, was based on the idea that night and the world below are in general closely related; it was also believed that at its setting the moon sank down into the lower world, so that a subterranean or gloomy Hecate (*Chthoniā*, *Skotiā*) was commonly recognized.

61. After the activity of these older forms had thus passed over into other spheres, **Selēnē**, or **Mēnē**, assumed the functions of the moon goddess proper, as Helios took the place of Apollo. Therefore in worship, which kept strictly to the ancient ideas, she stood quite in the background. In mythology her husband or lover is Endymion. He probably stands for the sun god who has entered into his cavern (ἐνδύω), *i.e.* the sun after it has set, with whom the moon goddess is united on the night of new moon. According to the Elean version of the myth she brought forth fifty daughters begotten by him, the representatives of the fifty months in the cycle of the Olympian games; but in the Carian myth the hunter, or herdsman, Endymion, was sleeping in a grotto of Mount Latmus, when Selene approached him by stealth, to kiss the beautiful sleeper.

62. The heroines Europa, Pasiphaë, and Antiope (the mother of Amphion and of Zethus) are to be regarded as representatives of Selene, and may, of course, be considered rivals of Hera. The Cretan-Boeotian **Europa** ('the wide-seeing'), daughter of Phoenix, or sister of Cadmus and daughter of Agenor and Telephassa ('the far-shining' moon goddess), was kidnaped on the shores of Sidon or Tyre by the bull-formed sun god Zeus *Asterios* (a divinity probably of Phoenician origin) and carried off to Crete, where she became the mother of Minos and Rhadamanthus. A Cretan also, and perhaps originally like her, is **Pāsiphaē** ('the one shining on all'), the daughter of Helios and Perseïs ('the glittering'). She became the mother of the Minotaurus, a monster which had the body of a man and the head of a bull. His father was the Cretan bull, *i.e.* the same bull-formed Zeus *Asterios*, whose worship was prominent at Gortyna, with whom king Minos also, the husband of Pasiphaë, must probably be identified.

63. In the most ancient times but few of the **stars** figured in mythology. The morning star, Heosphoros or Phosphorus ('light-bringer,' Lat. *Lūcifer*), is represented as a boy carrying a torch; the brilliant constellation Orion, as a giant hunter, with club raised aloft. Orion was carried off by Eos and killed by Artemis. His dog is Sirius ('the glittering'), the brightest of all the fixed stars, at whose rising the hottest time of the year, dog days, commences. The Bear looks anxiously around at Orion, and the rain goddesses, the starry group of the Pleiades, flee before his snares. Later, after the example of the Babylonians, all the individual groups of clear-shining stars were conceived of as picturesque figures, and by tales of metamorphoses were associated with the older mythical beings.

64. First among the light-divinities of another sort stands **Ēōs** ('dawn,' Lat. *Aurōra*), sister of Helios and Selene. As dispenser of the morning dew she carries pitchers in her hands. The brightness of the daily phenomenon which she represents caused to be attributed to her a saffron-yellow robe, arms and fingers beaming with rosy light, and glittering white wings. On account of her swiftness she is frequently represented riding in a chariot. Her husband was Tithonus, a brother of Priam; her son Memnon was killed by Achilles. As she had carried off Orion, so she stole **Tīthōnus** away when he was a beautiful youth, and obtained for him from Zeus the grant of immortality, but not of eternal youth. Therefore he withered away beside her, and as an old man, weakened by age, passed a miserable existence.

65. The swiftness with which the rainbow bends itself from heaven down to earth caused **Īris**, its representative, to be regarded as the messenger of the gods, so that large wings and a herald's staff (κηρύκειον) were attributed to her. In the older parts of the Iliad she appears as the messenger of Zeus; afterwards Hermes performs this function, while she serves Hera. As the rainbow was considered the harbinger of rainy weather, Iris was said to be wedded to Zephyrus, the rain wind. (See, further, Dioscuri, § 134.)

Apollo: Homer, Il. i. 9, 14: —
> Λητοῦς καὶ Διὸς υἱός,
> ἑκηβόλου 'Απόλλωνος, *et passim.*

Ovid, Her. viii. 83: —
> Apollinis arcus;

Met. i. 452 *sq.*, ii. 24; Vergil, Aen. iv. 376: —
> Augur Apollo,

et passim; Hyginus, Fab. clxi.; Shak., Love's Labour's Lost iv. 3, 343: —
> Bright Apollo's lute, strung with his hair.

Milton, Hymn on the Nativity 176: —
> Apollo from his shrine
> Can no more divine,
> With hollow shriek the steep of Delphos leaving.

Pope, Thebais i. 577: —
> Reveres Apollo's vocal caves;

i. 739: —
> But fir'd with rage, from cleft Parnassus' brow
> Avenging Phoebus bent his deadly bow.

Shak., Taming of the Shrew Ind. ii. 37, Antony and Cleopatra iv. 8, 29, King Henry VI. pt. iii. ii. 6, 11, Much Ado about Nothing v. 3, 25, Cymbeline ii. 3, 20, Hamlet iii. 2, 165, King Henry V. iv. 1, 289; Spenser, F. Q. i. i. 23, ii. 29, iv. 9.

Leto: Homer, Il. xxi. 489 *sq.;* Ovid, Met. vi. 160; Hyginus, Fab. cxl.; Keats, Endymion i. 861: —
> Hearken, sweet Peona!
> Beyond the matron-temple of Latona.

Python: Ovid, Met. i. 438 *sq.;* Hyginus, Fab. cxl.; Pope, Thebais i. 664: —
> When by a thousand darts the Python slain
> With orbs unroll'd lay cov'ring all the plain.

Aristaeus: Ovid, Fast. i. 363 *sq.*; Vergil, Geor. iv. 317 *sq.*

Hyacinthus: Ovid, Met. x. 185 *sq.*; Milton, Death of an Infant 23: —

> For so Apollo, with unweeting hand,
> Whilom did slay his dearly-loved mate,
> Young Hyacinth, born on Eurotas' strand,
> Young Hyacinth, the pride of Spartan land;
> But then transformed him to a purple flower,
> Alack, that so to change thee Winter had no power!

Phaëthon: Ovid, Met. ii. 34 *sq.*; Hyginus, Fab. clii., cliv.; Swift, Poem Suggested by the Hangings in Dublin Castle: —

> Finding, too late, he can't retire,
> He proves the real Phaëton,
> And truly sets the world on fire.

Pope, Weeping 13: —

> The Baby in that sunny sphere
> So like a Phaëton appears.

Shak., Two Gentlemen of Verona iii. 1, 153, King Henry VI. pt. iii. ii. 6, 12.

Artemis (Diana): Vergil, Aen. xi. 582: —

> Sola contenta Diana
> Aeternum telorum et virginitatis amorem
> Intemerata colit.

Ovid, Amor. iii. 2, 31, Her. iv. 87, Met. iii. 180 *sq.*; Horace, Car. Saec. 1; Hyginus, Fab. clxxxi.; Dryden, The Secular Masque 27: —

> With horns and with hounds I waken the day,
> And hie to the woodland walks away:
> I tuck up my robe, and am buskined soon,
> And tie to my forehead a wexing moon.

Pope, Summer 62: —

> And chaste Diana haunts the forest shade.

Shak., Midsummer Night's Dream i. 1, 89, Love's Labour's Lost iv. 2, 39, Titus Andronicus i. 1, 316, King Henry IV. pt. i. i. 2, 29; Spenser, F. Q. i. vii. 5; Chaucer, Knight's Tale 824.

Actaeon: Ovid, Met. iii. 174 *sq.*; Hyginus, Fab. clxxx.; Shak., Titus Andronicus ii. 3, 63.

Orion: Homer, Od. xi. 572; Ovid, Fast. v. 493 *sq.*; Vergil, Aen. i. 535; Hyginus, Fab. cxcv.; Cowper, Translation from Milton, To his Father: —

> Orion, soften'd, drops his ardent blade.

THE GREEK GODS 51

Cybele: Ovid, Ars Amat. i. 507; Vergil, Aen. iii. 111, xi. 768; Spenser, F. Q. i. vi. 15.
Amazones: Vergil, Aen. i. 490, v. 311, xi. 648 *sq.*; Hyginus, Fab. clxiii.
Hecate: Ovid, Fast. i. 141, Met. xiv. 405; Vergil, Aen. iv. 609; Greene, Fr. Bacon and Fr. Bungay ii. 176: —

> And hell and Hecate shall fail the friar.

Shak., Hamlet iii. 2, 269, King Lear i. 1, 112; Spenser, F. Q. i. i. 43.
Europa: Ovid, Her. iv. 55: —

> Juppiter Europen (primast ea gentis origo)
> Dilexit, tauro dissimulante deum;

Met. ii. 843 *sq.*; Hyginus, Fab. clxxviii.; Pope, Thebais i. 7: —

> Europa's rape, Agenor's stern decree.

Shak., Much Ado about Nothing v. 4, 45.
Minotaurus: Ovid, Ars Amat. ii. 24, Met. viii. 152 *sq.*; Vergil, Aen. vi. 25; Hyginus, Fab. xli., xlii.; Chaucer, Knight's Tale 122.
Eos (Aurora): The dawn goddess (Sanskrit USAS) is celebrated in 21 hymns of the Rig Veda. Praises are addressed to her for all the blessings of the light. So we find the sacredness of the dawn in the literature of Greece and Rome. Homer, Il. ii. 48: —

> Ἠὼς μέν ῥα θεὰ προσεβήσετο μακρὸν Ὄλυμπον.

Ovid, Met. iii. 149: —

> Altera lucem
> Cum croceis invecta rotis Aurora reducet;

Her. iii. 57, xvii. 112; Vergil, Aen. iv. 585: —

> Tithoni croceum linquens Aurora cubile;

Geor. iv. 544, Aen. iv. 7; Hyginus, Fab. clxxxiii.; Spenser, F. Q. i. ii. 7: —

> Now when the rosy-fingred morning faire
> Weary of aged Tithones' saffron bed;

xi. 51; Shak., Midsummer Night's Dream iii. 2, 380.
Tithonus: Ovid, Amor. ii. 5, 35, Fast. vi. 473.
Iris: Homer, Il. ii. *passim*; Ovid, Met. i. 271; Vergil, Aen. ix. 803; Milton, Comus 83: —

> These my sky-robes spun out of Iris' woof.

Shak., The Tempest iv. 1, 70.

II. THE DIVINITIES OF THE EARTH

66. It was probably at a later date than the development of most of the divinities thus far discussed, who embody forces operating in the sky and the air, that another series of real divinities grew up, out of the individual beings to whose activity were ascribed the forces operating on the earth itself in fire, water, and the fruit-bearing soil. The activity of these divinities was therefore now no longer confined to a particular spot and a single action; but they were believed to exert their power in a similar manner in all phenomena of the same sort.

1. The Goddess of Fire

67. Among these divinities, **Hestiā** ('hearth,' Lat. *Vesta*), the representative of the hearth fire, was in worship hardly distinguished at all, as a rule, from the element which she represented. To be sure, she took part in all sacrifices at which fire was necessary, but was seldom actually represented as an individual. When so represented, it was as a maiden clothed in a long garment and veiled, holding a dish or a scepter.

Hestia: See **Vesta** (after § 206).

2. Water Divinities

68. Most of the water divinities, likewise, remained always very closely associated with their element; only certain ones of them, — in particular, Poseidon, the ruler of the sea, and the Centauri ('Centaurs') and Sileni, — under the influence of worship, myth, and art, developed into richly-endowed personalities. **Ōceanus** is a mere personification of the ocean itself, which flows around the earth like a stream. From him were supposed to proceed not only springs, rivers, and seas, but also all other things, even the gods themselves, in harmony with the conceptions of the physical world adopted by the most ancient philosophers, which were suggested by the island-like situation of Greece. Therefore Oceanus was represented as a fatherly old man. He was said to live with his wife, Tethys ('nurse,' 'grandmother'), on the western border of the earth, without frequenting the assembly of the gods.

69. Somewhat like Oceanus, but more exactly characterized, was the **Halios Gerōn** ('old man of the sea'), who dwelt in a grotto deep down in the sea, and not only knew all the secrets of his element, but, like the sea gods of the Babylonians and the Germans, possessed inscrutable wisdom. But whoever wished to question him must first overpower him in a wrestling contest, and, in spite of his faculty for assuming various forms, like the water itself, must compel him to impart his knowledge.

From him were derived, differently named at different places, the sea gods Nereus ('flowing'), Proteus ('the firstborn'), and Phorcys, as well as Triton ('the streaming'), and Glaucus ('the glittering'). Of these the first three were represented in human form; Nereus and Proteus possessed the gift of prophecy and of changing their forms; while Phorcys and his wife Ceto ('sea monster') ruled over the sea monsters and other monsters. On the other hand, Halios Geron, Triton, and Glaucus, probably by association with Assyrio-

Babylonian prototypes of this sort of sea gods, prototypes which had reached Greece through the Phoenicians and Ionians, were, at a later period, still regularly represented as heterogeneous monstrosities in which a fish's belly was joined to the upper part of a human body, a shape that developed itself in the same way as the forms of the river gods, Centaurs, and Satyrs.

70. By the side of these lower sea divinities stand the **Nēreïdes**, *i.e.* daughters of Nereus, as representatives of the friendly forces operating in the sea, or, conceived of from the standpoint of the senses, as embodiments of the playful, bewitching waves. They were represented in the form of beautiful maidens, among whom Amphitrite ('the one streaming all around'), wife of Poseidon, Thetis, the mother of Achilles, and Galatea ('the milk-white one'), the shy maiden loved by the Cyclops Polyphemus, are especially prominent. Akin to them is **Īnō-Leucotheā**, whose aid was invoked in perils on the sea; for the Nereïds themselves are called also Leucotheae ('white goddesses'). In another aspect she became a secondary form of Aphrodite-Astarte, who is powerful on the sea, just as her son Melicertes was developed from the sun god and city god Melkart, of Tyre. Like Melkart, Melicertes was worshiped as a protector of sailors. Yet he was represented as a child in the arms of his mother, who, it was said, in a fit of madness had cast herself with him into the sea; sometimes, however, he appears standing upon a dolphin. His other name, Palaemon ('wrestler'), refers to his taking part in the celebration of the Isthmian games. He had a sanctuary in the neighborhood of Corinth, a city which had been an old Phoenician mart.

71. The destructive power of the threatening rocks and whirlpools in the sea was personified in the imaginary sea monsters **Scylla** and **Charybdis**. The former appears as a maiden, out of whose body grow six dogs' heads, which pull the rowers out of ships; but Charybdis is described by Homer in general only as a monster that three times a day sucks high water in. Both were in later times localized in the straits of Messina.

72. Of a more exalted nature than any of these beings is **Poseidōn** (Lat. *Neptūnus*), brother of Zeus and Hades. He is the ruler of the sea, and, at the same time, of all waters in general. As a symbol of his power, and as a weapon with which he can cleave the rocks and cut valleys in the mountains, he carries a trident, really a sort of harpoon which was used by fishermen in spearing dolphins and tunny. He was the national god of the Ionians, who lived chiefly by fishing and sailing the sea, just as his son Theseus was their national hero. Yet his worship is more ancient than that of Theseus; for as early as the Ionian migration it reached Asia, where the *Paniōnia* were celebrated in his honor on the promontory Mycale as a festival of the united Ionian colonies. To these corresponded in the fatherland the games established by Sisyphus and Theseus on the isthmus of Corinth, which were originally as purely Ionian as the old *Amphictyonia* ('sacrificial league') of Poseidon at Calaunia near Troezen. Sanctuaries of Poseidon were situated in many places, all over the Peloponnesus and on other coasts; but his dwelling place was said to be, with his wife Amphitrite, in a golden palace in the depths of the sea, near Aegae in Achaia.

73. As all springs and rivers flow from Oceanus, so Poseidon is the ruler of them all, evidently because it was supposed that they had a subterranean connection with the sea, which embraces all the land (*Gaiēochos*) and penetrates it. Earthquakes were thought to be caused by these subterranean waters, and Poseidon was therefore called the earth-shaker (*Ennosigaios*). So he was worshiped in many inland localities also, where inland lakes, rapid rivers, or earthquakes, seemed to prove the presence of his power, as was the case in Boeotia, Thessaly, and Arcadia. Yet, since he thus represented the fructifying moisture emanating from springs and rivers, he became also the protector of plant growth (*Phytalmios*), and therefore was associated with Demeter.

74. The animal usually sacrificed to Poseidon, which was likewise his symbol, was the horse; and so he rides along over the sea in a chariot drawn by dark horses with golden manes, whenever he commands the waves and winds. In the form of a horse (P. *Hippios*) he begot Arion, the battle horse of Adrastus, from an Erinys or Harpy, or by a thrust of his trident caused him to spring forth from a rock, just as in a similar manner in the contest with Athena he called into being a salt spring on the Acropolis of Athens.

75. Besides the horse, the bull (representing the wild might of the waves), and, in sharp contrast, the dolphin, which appears chiefly when the sea is quiet, are sacred and dear to Poseidon. In art, Poseidon is represented as similar to Zeus, only there appears in the features of the former less of the lofty repose than of the powerful might which the nature of his being calls for. Usually one foot is raised, a characteristic attitude of fishermen and sailors; in the works of art belonging to more ancient times he is entirely clothed, afterwards the upper part of his body is uncovered.

76. Like the waves of the sea, rapid rivers, by their ungovernable power, and their roaring, which resembles bellowing, gave rise to the idea that in every such stream a prodigious bull manifested his activity. Therefore in very ancient times the representations of **river gods** were formed like bulls, with a human countenance. But as early as the time of Homer, they appear in human form throughout; and only rarely does the later art indicate their nature by little bulls' horns, but usually makes them recognizable by the attribute of an urn. The most important of them are Acheloüs, the opponent of Hercules, and Alpheüs, the lover of the fountain nymph Arethusa, who fled before his wooing through the sea to the peninsula Ortygia at Syracuse. The most beautiful statue of a river god which can be definitely identified is that of the Nile, now in the Vatican museum.

77. The Centaurs and Sileni also were probably river gods, and may originally have come to be considered companions of Dionysus on account of the insatiable thirst implied by their nature; of course they are also very closely connected with him on account of the relation of water to the fruitfulness of the earth. The Aeolic-Thessalian **Centaurs**, sons of Ixion and Nephele ('cloud'), were natives of the mountains of Thessaly, particularly of Pelion and Ossa, also of Pholoë on the western border of Arcadia, and are probably to be regarded as embodiments of the wild, rushing streams of these mountains. So their origin is the cloud; they

rage, devastate tilled lands, carry off women (just as
Acheloüs and Alpheüs were ardent suitors), hurl rocks
and trees torn up by the roots, and hunt, *i.e.* surprise,
the wild animals hiding in the dry channels, and carry
them along with them. Like the waves of the sea, which
go swiftly raging by, they are represented as having
the form of a horse. In the oldest sculptures the hinder
part of a horse's body is simply joined to the back of
a complete human body; later, the human body near
the hips is represented as changing into the forequarters
of a horse, producing a formation which reminds one of
the shape of the river gods and Tritons. The Centaurs
fought (by inundations?) in the plains of Thessaly with
that mythical-historical people, the Lapithae ('stone-
men'). The Lapithae may be regarded as the builders
of the rocky citadels of Thessaly (and closely related
to the Phlegyae and Minyae), especially since the inhabitants of most of these localities venerated as their
founders heroes of the Lapithae with names similar to
those of the places themselves.

78. The king of the Lapithae was **Ixīŏn**, son of
Phlegyas. Ixion was regarded as the father of the
Centaurs. Because he had boasted of the favor of
Hera, Zeus caused him to be punished by being twisted
upon a swiftly-turning wheel in the lower world. He
was succeeded by his son Pirithoüs, the friend of Theseus. In consequence of their mania for drink, an idea
whose origin can be easily explained in the nature of
wild torrents, the Centaurs came into conflict with Hercules, as well as with Theseus and Pirithoüs, and in
such struggles were annihilated by those heroes. Quite
unlike the other Centaurs was Chiron ('the handy,'

'skillful'), who is probably to be considered as the representative of a brook that did not produce devastation. He dwelt in a cave on Mount Pelion, and was celebrated as a physician and prophet. (*Cf.* 'the old man of the sea,' § 69.) So he became the friend and tutor of the heroes Achilles, Jason, and Aesculapius, just as Silenus, the genius of the fountain, cared for the young Dionysus.

79. The **Silēnī** were Ionian-Phrygian gods of rivers and springs. Their bodies, like those of the Centaurs, were originally half man and half horse. As their chief representative appears the Silenus Marsyas, the god of the river rising at Celaenae in Phrygia. As the inventor of the Phrygian art of playing on the flute he was said to have challenged Apollo, the player of the lyre, to a contest, and, when vanquished by him, to have been flayed alive for his presumption. His skin was said to have been then inflated and hung up near his spring in Celaenae. Yet, as skins served as vessels for water, perhaps the skin was originally attributed to him, as the urn was to the river gods, only as a symbol of his character; and so possibly the story of this contest is to be regarded as a later invention to explain the attribute. In Athens the Sileni accompanying Dionysus were confused with the Peloponnesian Satyrs. The latter had the form of a goat, and about the time of Pisistratus had been introduced from Corinth as a feature of the festal songs and dances of the greater *Dionȳsia*.

80. The animating force of water was represented particularly by the **Nymphae** ('Nymphs'), who, being pictured to the imagination as young maidens or women, lightly clad, freely giving fruitfulness of all kinds,

appeared in every place where water exhibited a similar effect. This happened most naturally at the springs which had served as places for worship since most ancient times. The Naiades ('Naiads'), who represented such springs, were more exactly distinguished by mussel shells or other receptacles for water. But Nymphs were almost as frequent wherever an abundance of water produced luxuriant plant growth; and so the Oreades had their abode in the forests and pastures of the mountains. Moreover, the vital strength of every individual tree was explained as the activity of a soul-like nymph living in and together with it, who was designated as a Dryad ('tree nymph') or Hamadryad ('the one united with the tree'). Accordingly a nymph was supposed to live only so long as she was herself effective in the object whose vital power she represented. If the spring dried up, or the tree withered, the nymph also died. This kind of nymph marks an intermediate step between the divinities of water, and the special divinities of growth.

Oceanus: Hesiod, Theog. 133; Homer, Il. xiv. 246:—

'Ωκεανοῦ ὅς περ γένεσις πάντεσσι τέτυκται,

et passim; Ovid, Fast. v. 81; Hyginus, Fab. clxxxii.
Tethys: Homer, Il. xiv. 201:—

'Ωκεανόν τε θεῶν γένεσιν καὶ μητέρα Τηθύν.

Ovid, Met. ix. 499; Spenser, F. Q. i. iii. 31.
Nereus: Ovid, Amor. ii. 11, 39; Vergil, Aen. ii. 419; Horace, Od. i. 15, 5; Milton, Comus 871:—

By hoary Nereus' wrinkled look.

Spenser, F. Q. i. iii. 31.
Proteus: Homer, Od. iv. 365, 385 *sq.;* Ovid, Met. viii. 730 *sq.;* Vergil, Geor. iv. 429 *sq.;* Hyginus, Fab. cxviii.; Pope, Dunciad ii. 129:—

THE GREEK GODS

So Proteus, hunted in a nobler shape,
Became, when seiz'd, a puppy, or an ape.

Shak., King Henry VI. pt. iii. iii. 2, 192; Spenser, F. Q. i. ii. 10.

Triton: Hesiod, Theog. 931; Vergil, Aen. i. 144, x. 209; Ovid, Met. ii. 8; Milton, Comus 873: —

By scaly Triton's winding shell.

Shak., Coriolanus iii. 1, 89.

Glaucus: Ovid, Met. xiv. 9 *sq.*, Ibis 555; Milton, Comus 874: —

And old soothsaying Glaucus' spell.

Nereïdes: Homer, Il. xviii. 37 *sq.*; Ovid, Amor. ii. 11, 35, Met. xi. 361.

Amphitrite: Ovid, Met. i. 14; Keats, Endymion ii. 108: —

I would offer
All the bright riches of my crystal coffer
To Amphitrite.

Thetis: Homer, Il. i. 351, *et passim*, xviii. 35 *sq.*; Ovid, Met. xi. 221 *sq.*; Hyginus, Fab. liv.; Shak., Troilus and Cressida i. 3, 38, Pericles iv. 4, 41.

Ino (Leucothea): Homer, Od. v. 333; Hesiod, Theog. 976; Ovid, Met. iv. 488 *sq.*; Hyginus, Fab. ii., iv.

Melicertes (Palaemon): Ovid, Met. iv. 523 *sq.*; Hyginus, Fab. i., ii.

Charybdis; Scylla: Homer, Od. xii. 104 *sq.*; Ovid, Met. xiii. 730 *sq.*, Ibis 385; Vergil, Aen. i. 200, iii. 420; Milton, Par. L. ii. 1019: —

Or when Ulysses on the larboard shunn'd
Charybdis, and by the other whirlpool steer'd;

ii. 660: —

Vex'd Scylla bathing in the sea that parts
Calabria from the hoarse Trinacrian shore.

Poseidon (Neptunus): Hesiod, Theog. 15; Ovid, Epis. xviii. 129; Vergil, Geor. i. 14, Aen. i. 125 *sq.*; Hyginus, Fab. clvii.; Pope, Rape of the Lock v. 50: —

Blue Neptune storms, the bellowing deeps resound.

Shak., The Tempest v. 1, 35, Coriolanus iii. 1, 256, King Richard II. ii. 1, 63, Macbeth ii. 2, 60, Antony and Cleopatra ii. 7, 139; Spenser, F. Q. i. iii. 32, xi. 54.

Acheloüs: Ovid, Met. viii. 547 *sq.*
Alpheüs: Vergil, Aen. iii. 694: —

        Alpheum fama est huc Elidis amnem
Occultas egisse vias subter mare.

Ovid, Met. v. 599 *sq.*; Pope, Thebais i. 383: —

        Where first Alpheus hides
His wand'ring stream, and thro' the briny tides
Unmix'd to his Sicilian river glides.

Milton, Lycidas 132: —

    Return, Alpheus, the dread voice is past,
That shrunk thy streams.

Arethusa: Ovid, Met. v. 573 *sq.*; Vergil, Geor. iv. 344 *sq.*; Milton, Lycidas 85: —

    O fountain Arethuse, and thou honour'd flood.

Centauri (Centaurs): Hesiod, Shield of Herakles 178 *sq.*; Ovid, Met. xii. 210 *sq.*; Vergil, Aen. x. 195 *sq.*; Hyginus, Fab. xxxiii.; Pope, Vertumnus and Pomona 71; Spenser, F. Q. i. xi. 27.

Lapithae: Ovid, Met. xii. 250 *sq.*; Vergil, Geor. ii. 457; Hyginus, Fab. xxxiii.

Ixion: Pindar, Pyth. ii. 21-24; Vergil, Geor. iii. 38; Hyginus, Fab. lxii.; Pope, Ode on St. Cecilia's Day 67: —

    Ixion rests upon his wheel;

Rape of the Lock ii. 133; Spenser, F. Q. i. v. 35.

Phlegyas: Ovid, Met. v. 87; Vergil, Aen. vi. 618; Pope, Thebais i. 851: —

    In Phlegyas' doom thy just revenge appears,
Condemn'd to furies and eternal fears;
He views his food, but dreads, with lifted eye,
The mould'ring rock that trembles from on high.

Marsyas: Ovid, Met. vi. 382 *sq.*, Fast. vi. 707; Hyginus, Fab. clxv.

Naiades: Homer, Od. x. 350 *sq.*; Ovid, Fast. i. 405, Met. i. *passim*; Vergil, Ecl. x. 10, Geor. ii. *passim*, Aen. i. *passim*; Keats, Endymion ii. 690: —

        Art a maid of the waters,
One of shell-winding Triton's bright-hair'd daughters?

Pope, Fable of Dryope 18: —

    And to the Naiads flowery garlands brought.

Shak., The Tempest iv. 1, 128.

3. Divinities of Growth

81. The vital force that shows itself in the fruitfulness of the ground the ancients could not explain except on the hypothesis that such forces were to be traced to living beings, whose activity was patterned after the analogy of the reproduction of animals or human beings. Therefore it was assumed that in the ground were effective male and female divinities. With the former was associated the idea of fructifying moisture; with the latter, that of the reception and absorption of such moisture and the development of the seed into the plant. For the same reason fructification appears as an important element in the nature of those gods especially connected with water in the sky and on earth, the rain-bringers Zeus and Hermes, Poseidon, the river gods, and the Centaurs; and in the Satyrs, Pan, and Dionysus, this idea has embodied itself quite independently. On the other hand, Demeter, Gaea, and the originally foreign goddess, Rhea-Cybele (to whom the Ephesian Artemis and Aphrodite are akin), are goddesses of the receptive fruitfulness of the earth. The nymphs discussed above (§ 80) are very closely related to these goddesses.

82. The **Satyri** ('Satyrs') are the only individual divinities found, in more recent times, that originally belonged to the Peloponnesus. There the mountain districts were inhabited principally by goatherds, whose imagination embodied the fruitfulness of the earth in the form of the he-goat, because to them this animal naturally appeared to be the one especially adapted to produce fruitfulness. In their transition into human form, the Satyrs retained from this earlier stage of development the goat's ears and the little tail as symbols indicating their nature.

83. Closely allied to the Satyrs is the exclusively Arcadian shepherd god **Pān** ('the feeder'), whose father was the shepherd god Hermes, and whose mother was a daughter of Dryops, *i.e.* a Dryad. For, like the Satyrs, he is represented in the form of a he-goat, and so may probably be considered merely a type of these fructifying divinities, who was transformed by the imagination of the Arcadian shepherds into a divine shepherd. First of all he produces fruitfulness and increase of the flocks. Moreover, like the shepherds themselves, in the summer he dwells in the rocky caves of the mountains, and in the winter descends into the plains. In the heat of midday he rests, at evening he plays the shepherd's flute (*sȳrinx*); and as accessory employments he carries on hunting, fishing, and war. Yet it is he that inspires in the flocks, and likewise in their masters, sudden fright ('panic'), hurrying them along into unreasoning flight. His love for the moon goddess Selene is probably to be explained by the fact that moonshine assures to the flocks a favorable pasturage, fresh with dew.

84. His worship spread from Arcadia by the way of Argolis and Athens to Parnassus and even to Thessaly. In later times, on account of the relation between his nature and that of Dionysus, he came to be looked upon as an attendant of that god, probably by being associated with the Satyrs. Finally, the theorizing of the philosophers, by changing the signification of his name (making τὸ πᾶν = 'the universe'), and by comparing him to the great goat-shaped god of Mendes, in Egypt, transformed him into a great, all-powerful ruler and pervading spirit of the life of nature as a whole, at whose death all this life of nature dies away. He was represented as bearded, with the legs, tail, ears, and horns of a he-goat; often, however, in human form, distinguished only by the animal-like expression of his face.

85. Dionȳsus (Lat. *Bacchus*) himself, the most important of these divinities of fruitfulness, was once represented in animal form, namely, that of a bull, richly endowed with procreative power, as is seen from certain of the customs of his worship in Argos and Elis; and at a later period the bull and the he-goat were still considered the most acceptable offerings to him. Nevertheless, the worship of Dionysus ('Zeus-man' or 'Zeus-hero') had its origin, properly speaking, in Thrace; and from there, by an emigration of part of the inhabitants toward the southwest, it reached Phocis and Boeotia, and, later, Attica also. The Phocians were closely related to the Phrygians of Asia Minor, among whom he was worshiped, under the name *Sabāzius*, as son of Ma, the mother of the gods.

86. In his native home, and later also in Greece, the worship of the god was celebrated by women, who in sensual ecstasy, carrying torches, reveled by night through the mountain forests in so-called 'orgies,' a word that is connected with ὀργάω ('to swell with fructifying moisture'). These devotees of his became in mythology sometimes his nurses, the nymphs, and sometimes his attendants, the Bacchae ('exulting ones'), Maenades ('raving ones'), and Thyiades ('raging ones'). To fill themselves (and typically, at the same time, the rural districts represented by them) with new procreative power, they tore in pieces young animals (and, in the earliest times, probably even children) which

F

had been dedicated to the god, and which, according to the older idea, filled his place. Then they drank the blood, which was regarded as the seat of vital strength, devoured the raw flesh, and wrapped themselves in the fresh skin. At the same time with a loud voice they besought the god (whom at the time of the winter solstice fancy pictured as a sleeping child in a winnowing fan) to dispense fruitfulness in the year just beginning. The god was called also Bacchus or Iacchus from the shouts uttered by them.

87. It was for the same purpose that in the rural districts of Attica the *phallus* was carried about during the lesser *Dionȳsia*, which came at the same time in the year (*Poseideōn* = December-January). In Athens itself, at the festival of the *Anthestēria* ('flower festival'), this favor of the god was sought by the ceremony of his symbolic marriage with a queen representing the soil. In the times of the republic her place was filled by the wife of the *Archōn Basileus*.

88. As the bull and the he-goat, of all the animals, were especially sacred to Dionysus, so in the vegetable kingdom were the evergreen ivy and the vine swelling with juice, on account of their luxuriant growth. The **vine** was especially appropriate also for the reason that the enjoyment of wine drinking has the faculty of increasing the sensual excitement peculiar to this worship to a point of enthusiasm that is like madness (drunkenness). (*Cf.* 'Spirit,' 'spirits of wine.') Such an effect, moreover, corresponded to the nature of Dionysus, who was so generally believed to be taken into oneself in drink that his relation to wine gradually drove into the background all other phases of his character. As *Lyaeus* ('freer from care') he carries for a symbol the vine branch or the *thyrsus* (vine-prop?). In his honor was celebrated at Athens the vintage festival of the *Oschophoria* ('carrying about of vines'), as well as the *Lēnaea* ('feast of the wine press'); while on the island of Naxos, which abounded in wines, and was the center of the worship of Dionysus among the islands having an Ionian population, the *dīthyrambus* was probably first sung. This was originally a simple drinking song in honor of the god, which in Corinth became a chorus rendered by singers in the costume of Satyrs. From this was developed the dithyramb of Pindar at the festivals of Dionysus in Thebes. In Athens, however, it became the drama, at first in the form of 'tragedy' ($\tau\rho\alpha\gamma\omega\delta\acute{\iota}\alpha$ = 'goat song') or satyr-play. Here, at the spring games of the greater *Dionȳsia*, the presentation of the dramas that grew out of the dithyramb came at length to constitute the most essential part of the festival.

89. When the real significance of the above-mentioned sacrifice of children was no longer understood, the Orphic poets, *i.e.* the representatives of the religious poetry developed by the worship of Dionysus, about the time of Pisistratus, attempted to explain that sacrificial custom by inventing the story that Dionysus himself, when a child, or in animal form, had been torn in pieces by the Titans, and had therefore received the name *Zagreus.* There was, however, symbolized in that fable an idea based on an actual process of nature; for Dionysus really seemed to die in the fall. As the reproductive power of nature vanishes after the harvest time for a season, so its awakening in the spring, which in Athens was celebrated by the *Anthestēria* ('flower festival'), could be looked upon as a resurrection of the fructifying god, and thus he could easily be regarded as having been temporarily dead. This was the case particularly at Delphi, and probably also in the 'mysteries' of Eleusis.

90. When this Thracian 'Zeus-hero' and representative of productive moisture was introduced into the Grecian system of gods, he came to be regarded as the son of Zeus, the god of thunder and rain; and his mother Semele (Earth?) was said to be the daughter of Cadmus of Thebes, because that was the chief place of his worship. After her premature death, continued the legend, Zeus concealed the yet immature child in his own thigh till the time for it to be born. Then Hermes carried it to the nymphs of Nysa, or the synonymous Hyades ('raincloud goddesses') to be nursed.

91. Certain other myths relate to the opposition which was raised to the introduction of this foreign worship. Even in Thrace, the very home of the god, barbarian opponents of his worship were personified in Lycurgus, who pursued him and his nurses with a battle-ax. In the Minyan Orchomenus he was resisted by the soberly industrious daughters of Minyas, similarly in Argos by the daughters of Proetus, and in Thebes by king Pentheus; but these all perished when the god sent upon them the madness which sensual excitement finally reaches.

92. The legend of the marriage of Dionysus with Ariadne, a Cretan goddess very much like Aphrodite, which was localized on the island of Naxos (Dia) near Crete, is entirely in harmony with the nature of the fructifying god; and the significance of this wedlock is indicated by the names of their sons, Oenopion ('wine-drinker'), Staphylus ('grape-cluster'), and Euanthes ('the richly blooming'). He is, however, associated with Aphrodite as the father of Priapus, god of gardens and flocks, who was worshiped at Lampsacus on the Hellespont and was essentially like his father.

93. The oldest symbol of the worship of Dionysus is a consecrated post or pillar (the idea of which probably arose from a sacred tree); and from this, by the addition of a mask and clothing, the oldest regular images naturally developed. The type of the god in which he is bearded and fully clothed was the prevalent one till sometime during the fourth century B.C.; later he appeared as a child on the arm of Hermes or of a bearded Satyr. After Praxiteles represented him as a youth nearly nude, clothed only with a skin of a fawn, the nude and youthful form came to be universally accepted.

94. Among the goddesses of the receptive fruitfulness of the earth, a prominent place was occupied by **Dēmētēr** (*cf.* μήτηρ, Lat. *Cerēs*), the protectress of grain, which is the chief means of subsistence. Her parents were supposed to be Cronus, the sun god, who ripens the produce of the fields, and Rhea, whose nature is closely related to her own. Her epithets, *Chloē* ('green-yellow'), *Karpophoros*, *Sītō*, and *Iūlō* ('dispenser of fruit, grain, sheaves'), signify that she is the protectress of the germinating seed; and this idea is confirmed by the fact that the first fruits of the harvest were offered to her.

95. Her principal residence was in Eleusis near Athens, where, with **Corē** ('girl'), her daughter by Zeus, and with the youthful Iacchus, *i.e.* Dionysus-Bacchus-Sabazius (whose worship was probably introduced into this cult originally at Athens), she was worshiped in public and in secret ceremonies ('Mysteries'). Dionysus was here considered sometimes the son of Demeter, and again of Core and the Zeus of the lower world, *i.e.* Hades. The two goddesses were together termed 'honorable,' or 'mistresses.' In the month Boëdromion (September-October) of each year the people of Athens marched along the sacred road to Eleusis in a festal procession, in which sheaves of grain were carried in token of thanks that the promise of the harvest was fulfilled. Here, in the darkness of the night, a torchlight procession took place, which probably stood originally for the renewal of the light in spring, but was at a later period explained by the idea that Demeter had searched for her stolen daughter by torchlight. The sacred symbols of the goddess were exhibited to the initiated (*Mystae*); and to remind them of the beneficence shown by her toward men in distributing grain, there was offered them after long fasting a drink, or pap, of water and meal seasoned with pennyroyal, the form in which, at least in the earliest times, the gifts of Demeter had been enjoyed. (*Cf.* the *puls* of the Romans.) Finally water was poured out (as a charm for rain), while, with eyes looking toward the heavens, they cried, ὖε ('rain!'); and, looking toward the ground, κύε ('conceive!').

As a preliminary to these greater Mysteries, the lesser Mysteries were celebrated in Athens itself in the flowering month Anthesterion (February–March), an occasion on which those that were to be received as members of the religious community in the fall had a provisional initiation.

96. In Homer, too, Demeter, 'of the beautiful ringlets,' who is the wife of Zeus, and is worshiped in the Thessalian Pyrasus ('land of wheat'), is only the goddess of the cultivation of grain, so that she seems to dwell not on Olympus, but in the grainfield itself. The sacred hymn containing her legendary history, a hymn composed in Attica before the time of Solon, represents her in the same way: — 'Core, her daughter by Zeus, is gathering flowers together with the Oceaninae, *i.e.* the daughters of Oceanus, in a meadow situated, according to the later version, near Enna in Sicily. When, among other flowers, she plucks the flower of death, the narcissus, suddenly the ground opens (*cf.* the German *Schlüsselblume*, *Himmelsschlüssel*), and Hades, the lord of the world below, rises up out of it, and carries her away from the circle of her playmates. Without tasting food, her mother, torches in hand, searches for her for nine days, until from Hecate or Helios she learns who has kidnaped the girl. When Zeus denies her request for the restoration of her child, Demeter hides herself in Eleusis, and in anger prevents the growth of all grain. Not until Zeus, in consequence of this action on her part, has at length decided that Core shall remain but a third part of each year in the lower world does the goddess return to Olympus and again give fruitfulness to the grain. The refusal of a complete restoration is confirmed by the fact that Core has taken from her husband, and eaten, the seed of a pomegranate (a symbol of fructification).'

97. This legend plainly typifies the development of the seed itself, for in the earliest times in Greece, according to Hesiod, grain was mostly sown in the spring, so that it was in the ground four months, from about the beginning of March to the beginning of July, and here it was fructified; but with the harvest it was separated from the ground eight months. Moreover, among all the Indo-European races there is found an intimate connection between the concepts 'child' and 'grain,' between human fructification and the fruitfulness of the grainfield; hence the effort was made to express the latter idea by symbolic actions, and by forms of speech properly referring to the former, which were apparently indecent. Thus, according to the Cretan myth, Iasion begets from Demeter, on a thrice-plowed cornfield, Plutus, *i.e.* abundance of fruit, wealth. It is, however, a charming legend in which Demophoön, the little, sickly son of Celeüs, king of Eleusis, under the nourishment of the goddess, flourishes like the germinating seed. Very closely related to him stands another of her Eleusinian protégés, the hero Triptolemus ('the one plowing thrice'), who was worshiped as the first propagator of agriculture and the founder of the Eleusinian cult. Demeter sends him abroad, furnished with seed corn and agricultural implements, on her own chariot drawn by serpents, to teach men agriculture and the milder civilization and political order following in the wake of agriculture. Therefore Demeter herself was revered as *Thesmophoros* ('law-giver'), particularly at the festival of the *Thesmophoria* celebrated in the month of seedtime.

98. In Arcadia Demeter was associated with Poseidon *Hippios* or *Phytalmios*, and her daughter was there called *Despoina* ('mistress'). The latter, as wife of Hades, became also **Persephonē** ('the ravaging destroyer'), *i.e.* the dread goddess of death and the mistress of the lower world, while, in harmony with her mythical character, she seems to have been worshiped in the Mysteries as a consoling example of one who experienced a resurrection and a happy after-life in the lower world.

In the older art no fixed form was developed for Demeter except that she was always represented as motherly and fully clothed. As distinguishing attributes she carries ears of corn and the poppy, a scepter or a torch. Her daughter is distinguished from her only by her youthful, maidenly figure; and the two are often seen side by side, sitting or standing.

99. The nourishing earth in its totality is represented by **Gaea** or **Gē** (Lat. *Tellūs* or *Terra Māter*). She is the broad-breasted, great mother of all, who produces men, animals, and plants, and hence was worshiped in Athens as *Kūrotrophos* ('nurse of children'). But because she also receives back into her bosom all that die she is likewise goddess of death. She knows the secrets of the realm of death, which lies in the earth, and so she was consulted as an oracular goddess, especially at chasms in the ground, which seemed to lead down to that realm, particularly at Aegae in Achaia. The real belief probably was that she sent up the dead themselves to be consulted. As *Kūrotrophos* she is represented sitting and holding children and fruits in her lap; at her feet cattle and sheep are feeding. Far more frequently, however, she is represented as a gigantic woman, with only the upper part of her body in view, rising up out of the ground; more rarely, with only the head appearing. In the latter form she is usually handing over her son Erichthonius to Athena to be brought up. In later times she is reclining on the ground, holding a cornucopia; and this conception is the one followed in the personifications of various countries, islands, and cities, the last of which are frequently more definitely denoted by a mural crown.

Satyri: Ovid, Fast. iii. 737 *sq.*, Ars Amat. iii. 157; Vergil, Ecl. v. 73; Spenser, F. Q. i. vi. 18.

Pan: Homer, Hymn xix.; Ovid, Met. i. 699 *sq.*; Hyginus, Fab. cxcvi.; Milton, Par. L. iv. 266: —

>   While universal Pan
> Knit with the Graces and the Hours in dance
> Led on th' eternal Spring.

Pope, Summer 50: —

> Rough Satyrs dance and Pan applauds the song.

Keats, Endymion i. 78: —

> Where fed the herds of Pan.

Wordsworth, Sonnet v.: —

> Great Pan himself low whispering through the reeds.

Dionysus (Bacchus, Iacchus, Lyaeus): Ovid, Ars Amat. i. 232: —

> Purpureus Bacchi cornua pressit Amor;

Met. iii. 317, iv. 2 *sq.*; Vergil, Aen. i. 734: —

> Laetitiae Bacchus dator.

Hyginus, Fab. clxxix.; Shak., Antony and Cleopatra ii. 7, 121: —

> Come, thou monarch of the vine,
> Plumpy Bacchus with pink eyne!
> In thy fats our cares be drown'd,
> With thy grapes our hairs be crown'd!

Semele: Homer, Il. xiv. 323; Ovid, Met. iii. 260 *sq.*, Fast. vi. 485; Hyginus, Fab. clxxix.

Hyades: Ovid, Fast. iv. 678, v. 164; Vergil, Aen. i. 744; Hyginus, Fab. cxcii.

Pentheus: Ovid, Met. iii. 513 *sq.*; Vergil, Aen. iv. 469; Hyginus, Fab. clxxxiv.

Ariadne: Catullus, lxiv. 251 *sq.*; Ovid, Fast. iii. 473; Hyginus, Fab. xlii., xliii.; Keats, Endymion ii. 442: —

>   Never, I aver,
> Since Ariadne was a vintager.

Shak., Midsummer Night's Dream ii. 1, 80.

Priapus: Ovid, Fast. i. 415 *sq.*; Vergil, Ecl. vii. 33; Shak., Pericles iv. 6, 3.

Demeter (Ceres): Homer, Od. v. 125; Ovid, Amor. iii. 10, 11: —
> Prima Ceres docuit turgescere semen in agris;

Fast. iv. 393 *sq.*, Met. x. 431; Vergil, Geor. i. 7, 96; Pope, Windsor Forest 39: —
> Here Ceres' gifts in waving prospect stand.

Shak., The Tempest iv. 1, 60.

Narcissus: Ovid, Met. iii. 346 *sq.*; Shak., Rape of Lucrece 38.
Plutus: Shak., All's Well That Ends Well v. 3, 101.
Triptolemus: Hyginus, Fab. cxlvii.
Persephone (Proserpina): Homer, Hymn to Ceres; Ovid, Met. v. 385 *sq.*, Fast. iv. 485; Vergil, Geor. iv. 487; Hyginus, Fab. cxlvi.; Keats, Lamia i. 63: —
> As Proserpine still weeps for her Sicilian air.

Milton, Par. L. iv. 269: —
> Where Proserpin gathering flow'rs
> Herself a fairer flower by gloomy Dis
> Was gather'd, which cost Ceres all that pain
> To seek her through the world.

Shak., Troilus and Cressida ii. 1, 37; Spenser, F. Q. i. i. 37: —
> Blacke Plutoes griesly dame;

iv. 11: —
> Queen of Hell.

III. DIVINITIES OF THE LOWER WORLD

1. Divinities of Death

100. As the divinities of the upper world were patterned entirely after living human beings, so the god to whom in the time of Homer was attributed a power (corresponding to that of Zeus) over the lower world and its inhabitants was formed in harmony with those ideas about the dead which have been explained above. (See

§ 2 *sq.*) Like his subjects, he is invisible, and hence is called Aïdoneus, Aïdes, or **Hādēs**, 'the invisible,' or 'the one rendering invisible' (ἀ privative + ἰδ-εῖν). This peculiarity is ascribed to the power of a helmet which he is accustomed to wear. A similar helmet is used by Siegfried in the *Niebelungenlied*.

The all-powerful ruler of the lower world was considered the brother of Zeus and Poseidon; indeed, he was himself called the subterranean (*Chthonios*) Zeus, and like him is represented enthroned, with a scepter.

101. His wife is Persephoneia or Persephone, and like her, Hades is both ruler of the depths of the earth and protector of the grain as long as it rests in the bosom of the earth. Regarded in this aspect he carried the horn of plenty as a symbol, and was much worshiped under the names *Plūtō* ('giver of riches,' Lat. *Dīs Pater*), *Clymenus* ('the illustrious'), and *Eubūleus* ('the benevolent'); while as the death god proper, Hades, he enjoyed worship especially at Pylus ('gate' of the lower world) in Elis. When praying to him it was customary to strike on the ground with the hands, that the god might hear; and black sacrificial animals were offered to him, as to the dead themselves. The dark-hued cypress, which was planted on graves and otherwise much employed in the worship of the dead, and the quickly withering narcissus were sacred to him. The Erinyes, Thanatos, and Hypnos, god of sleep, who is formed like Thanatos, dwell in his realm. (Concerning his wound at the hand of Hercules see § 143.)

Hades (Pluto): Homer, Il. *passim;* Vergil, Geor. iv. 467, *et passim;* Horace, Od. ii. 14, 7; Milton, Il Penseroso 107: —

> Drew iron tears down Pluto's cheek,
> And made Hell grant what love did seek.

Pope, Song by a Person of Quality v.: —
> Gloomy Pluto, King of terrors,
> Arm'd in adamantine chains.

Shak., King Henry IV. pt. ii. ii. 4, 169; Chaucer, Knight's Tale 1224, *et passim;* Spenser, F. Q. i. iv. 11.

Hypnos: Daniel, Delia, Sonnet li.; Tennyson, In Memoriam lxvii.

2. Divinities of Sickness and Healing

102. Since the death divinities possess power over life and death, when propitiated they may become health divinities, who ward off sickness and death. To those who seek help and healing they make known their will and counsel mostly by oracular dreams, just as the dead themselves are wont to appear to their friends in dreams. So **Aesculapius** (Gk. *Asklēpios*), the most important of them, was an oracular god, closely related to Hades, probably at first indigenous to the vicinity of the Thessalian town Tricca at the foot of Mount Pindus. He was believed to dwell in the depths of the earth, and therefore, like the dead, was represented in the form of a serpent. His priests, however, the family of the Asclepiadae, practiced the actual art of healing as an occult science, so that the remedies which were apparently prescribed by the god had the desired effect. They transplanted into Boeotia the worship of Aesculapius as the god of healing, where it was combined with the similar worship of Trophonius at Lebadia. Afterwards they carried it also into Phocis and Epidaurus in Argolis. From there it reached Rome in the year 291 B.C.

103. In Homer, on the other hand, Aesculapius has already reached the lower level of a mere medical hero;

he is the son of Apollo, the god of healing, but is instructed in the healing art by the wise Centaur, Chiron. Since by his art he even calls back the dead to life, the god of the lower world complains of him to Zeus, and the latter thereupon slays him with a stroke of lightning. His children are the physicians Machaon and Podalirius, and the personifications of health and healing, Hygea ('health'), Iaso ('healing'), Panacea ('cure-all,' 'remedy for everything'), and Aegle ('the shining one,' 'the wonderful'). Aesculapius is usually represented as a kindly, wise-looking man, standing, and with all the upper part of his body bare, except the left arm and shoulder. He carries as a symbol a large staff, entwined with a serpent, and often wears a headband.

Aesculapius: Homer, Il. iv. 194; Hyginus, Fab. xlix.; Shak., Pericles iii. 2, 111: —
    And Aesculapius guide us!
Spenser, F. Q. i. v. 41.
 Machaon: Homer, Il. ii. 732; Ovid, Ex Pont. i. 3, 5.
 Aegle: Vergil, Ecl. vi. 21: —
    Aegle, Naiadum pulcherrima.
Shak., Midsummer Night's Dream ii. 1, 79.

IV. PERSONIFICATIONS

104. As men's conception of the gods gradually becomes spiritualized, such forces as are not directly perceptible through the senses, but are rather of a purely spiritual nature, whose effect is manifest as well in private as in public life, are attributed to the activity of independent divinities. Thus that which we know as a mere abstract idea acquires a personal form. So are developed (1) the friendly divinities of love, social intercourse, order, and justice; (2) the hostile divinities of war and strife; (3) the divinities of fate, who determine all that happens to man. Closely related to the genuine personifications of these spiritual forces are those attributes of older divinities of nature which have been developed into independent figures (*e.g.* Athena-Nike). And in the case of some of these very divinities of nature (*e.g.* Aphrodite and Ares), even in foreign lands before their reception into the circle of the Greek gods, purely spiritual functions came so prominently into the foreground as almost entirely to supplant their older signification in the natural world. It was not until a comparatively late period that a similar result followed with such indigenous divinities as the Charites and Horae.

1. THE DIVINITIES OF LOVE, SOCIAL INTERCOURSE, ORDER, AND JUSTICE

105. In Greece **Aphroditē** (Lat. *Venus*) was preëminently the goddess of love and of the beauty that inspires love. When in Homer she is derided by her sister Athena on account of her unwarlike nature, Zeus himself, smiling gently, comes to her defense with the explanation, —

> Not upon thee were bestowed, dear daughter, the deeds of war;
> Order thou rather, as ever, the delightful affairs of marriage.

So Eros, love's longing personified, is regarded as her constant companion, and according to the later idea, as her son. In their train are found Peitho ('persuasion') and the Charites, to whom Aphrodite is otherwise closely related; for in the Iliad Charis is the wife of Hephaestus, while according to the Odyssey Aphrodite herself occupies this position. Her parents were Zeus and Dione; while Hebe, the representative of the bloom of youth, was the daughter of Zeus and Hera. In Thebes Aphrodite was considered the wife of Ares, god of war and death, with whom she is associated in Homer. Their children were Harmonia ('harmony') — who resembles Aphrodite herself when the latter is called *Pandēmos* ('common to all,' and therefore 'unifying') — and the companions of the war god, Deimos ('terror') and Phobos ('fright').

106. These rather vague relations and the fact that Aphrodite appears to take the place of other goddesses (see also § 117) indicate that she is not indigenous to Greece. As she is in Homer frequently called 'the Cyprian' (*Kypris*), and as the cities where her worship appears to have been first carried on, Paphos, Amanthus, and Idalium, were situated in Cyprus, probably her original home was on this island. From here her worship could afterwards easily have reached Cythera and Sparta, Corinth, Elis, and Athens, and, in the other direction, Mount Eryx in Sicily. Even in Cyprus, however, she was probably only a local form of the Assyrio-Phoenician goddess of fruitfulness, Istar or Astarte (Ashtoreth = Aphrodet?). Their identity appears especially in their relation to the Semitic representative of the vegetation of the springtime, **Adōnis** ('lord'), who was worshiped principally in the Syrian town Byblus and in Cyprus. Fancy pictured him as a handsome youth, beloved of Aphrodite, wounded in the chase in midsummer by a wild boar (the sun). He dies immediately, and is then compelled to pass the time till spring in the lower world with Persephone, who is his Greek counterpart.

107. To Cyprus belonged originally also the myth of the double-sexed **Aphrodītos** or **Hermaphrodītus**, a representative of the abundant productiveness of nature, closely akin to Aphrodite. The latter of his names was probably given him only because representations of him were usually in the form of *Hermae*. Through a mistaken explanation of this name, he was afterwards supposed to be a son of Hermes and Aphrodite (*cf.* Priapus). The legend of Aphrodite's union with **Anchīsēs**, king of Dardanus in Troas, whom she approached on Mount Ida and to whom she afterwards bore **Aenēās**, is likewise of oriental origin. Possibly Anchises and the son of Priam, the handsome Paris, who awards her the prize for beauty, may be as nearly identical as are Aphrodite and the beautiful Helen, whom she gives Paris as a reward for his decision.

108. Even the customary appellation of the goddess in worship, *Ūraniā* ('the heavenly'), seems to have been borrowed from Astarte. For the idea that Aphrodite was a daughter of Uranus was evidently first invented in explanation of that appellation, and was based upon a false explanation of her epithet 'foam-born.' Similarly, her relation to the sea cannot be explained from her significance in Greece, nor can her worship as *Euploia* ('bestower of a prosperous voyage'), *Pontiā* ('sea goddess'), and the like, in which capacity the dolphin and the swan are her symbolic attributes.

109. In earlier times Aphrodite, like all the other goddesses, was represented clothed; but after the fourth century B.C. she appears also half-nude, or entirely so, since she was conceived of as bathing, or as *Anadyomenē* ('emerging from the sea'). The most beautiful example of a semi-nude Aphrodite is the famous Aphrodite of Melos. Praxiteles represented her as entirely undressed in the statue made for her sanctuary in Cnidus. As symbols of fruitfulness the dove, ram, or he-goat are her special attributes.

110. Erōs, on the other hand, was the masculine representative of love. He was worshiped as a real god from ancient times, probably even by the prehellenic population of Thespiae in Boeotia, Parion on the Hellespont, and Leuctra in Laconia. At Thespiae he was worshiped under the very ancient symbol of a rough stone; but he was there considered the son of Hermes, the dispenser of fruitfulness, and of the Artemis of the lower world (a goddess of earth's fruitfulness, much like Demeter and Persephone). In the Homeric poems, however, he does not yet appear as a divinity; and Hesiod, though certainly acquainted with his actual worship, regards him only as a world-engendering primitive force.

111. Hīmeros (Lat. *Cupīdō*), the longing of impetuous love, and **Pothos**, love's ardent desire, were after a while distinguished from Eros; but they were not recognized as actual divinities. Thus there was gradually developed a plurality of Erotes not easily distinguished from each other. After the beginning of the fifth century B.C. Eros was represented in art as a winged boy or a youth of tender years, with a flower and a lyre, a fillet (*taenia*) and a garland in his hands, often in company with Aphrodite, who now was regarded as his mother. After the fourth century B.C. he received as attributes a bow and arrow, and also a torch; for love's smart which he inflicted was regarded as a wound. Still later, through a misunderstanding, the torch was supposed to symbolize the light of life, and Eros, like Aphrodite, was associated also with death and the lower world. The torch in his hand was reversed or extinguished, and sometimes he was represented as fatigued and just sinking down to sleep; thus he became practically identical with Thanatos, the god of death.

Finally, the Platonic conception, that love both blesses and curses and torments the human soul, was expressed by representing Eros as now flatteringly embracing, and again cruelly torturing Psyche ('soul'), who was pictured as a butterfly (§ 4), or as a maiden with a butterfly's wings.

112. The **Charites** (Lat. *Grātiae*, Eng. 'Graces'), the goddesses of charming grace, were adored in the Boeotian city, Orchomenus, under the symbol of three rough stones, a symbol which, like the stone of Eros in Thespiae, may have had its origin in the times preceding the dominion of the Minyae. In other localities, even in very ancient times, they were represented as three maidens, clothed in long robes, standing in single file, with instruments of music, or with flowers, fruits, and fillets, in their hands. In this type they cannot be distinguished from Muses or Nymphs. In Athens, after the fifth century B.C., they were usually united in a group, clasping each other's hands; but not until the third century were they represented as entirely nude and embracing each other.

113. In the Iliad the individual divinity Charis is the wife of Hephaestus; but Homer is acquainted with a whole family of Charites. Usually Zeus was considered their father, and Eurynome ('the wide-ruling one'), a daughter of Oceanus, as their mother. Their names are usually Euphrosyne ('cheerfulness'), Thalia ('bloom of life,' 'festal banquet'), and Aglaïa ('brightness'). By these names they are shown to have been goddesses of cheerful sociability, though they may have originally embodied particularly the glad charm of spring, and may have been closely related to the Horae.

114. The predilection of the Graces for the round dance and its accompanying music was shared by the **Mūsae** ('the searchers,' or 'inventors,' Eng. 'Muses'). They were the daughters of Zeus and Mnemosyne ('memory'), and were worshiped (especially on Olympus in the district of Pieria, and on Helicon in Boeotia) at sacred springs, such as Aganippe and Hippocrene on Helicon, and Castalia on Parnassus, in connection with the worship of Dionysus and Apollo and the singer Orpheus, the representative of the Dionysiac poetry. In the Iliad and the older parts of the Odyssey their number is not yet fixed; but in a more recent part of the latter poem, and in Hesiod, they are, as is usual in literature, nine in number. It was not, however, until later times that their individual functions were more specifically determined as follows: Calliope ('the beautiful-voiced'), as the muse of heroic (epic) poetry, carries writing tablets and a style; Clio ('she that praises') represents history and has a written scroll; Euterpe ('the charmer'), lyric poetry, a double flute; Thalia ('joy of life'), comedy, a comic mask; Melpomene ('the singer'), tragedy, a tragic mask, and sometimes a sword; Terpsichore ('joyful in the dance'), dancing, a lyre; Urania ('the heavenly'), astronomy, a celestial globe; Erato ('the beloved'), love songs, a cithara; finally, Polymnia or Polyhymnia ('rich in hymns') attends to the songs of divine worship, and therefore appears veiled and with garments drawn closely about her.

115. The **Hōrae**, as their name implies, were representatives of the seasons; and as in earlier times only three seasons were distinguished, there were three corresponding Horae, represented as maidens in the bloom of youth. In Attica they were named Thallo ('the blooming one'), Carpo ('the fruit-bringer'), and, perhaps, Auxo ('the increaser'). In Homer they open and shut the gates of heaven, *i.e.* they gather and disperse the clouds. Afterwards, also, they were considered the dispensers of rain and dew. In art the regularity of the recurrence of the seasons was expressed by representing the Horae as engaged in the dance. This, too, made them appear as protectresses of order; and so they were named also Eunomia ('good order'), Dike ('justice'), and Irene ('peace'). Irene was extensively worshiped in Athens as an individual divinity; rising above the market place stood a bronze statue of her, made by Cephisodotus. She was represented holding on her arm the child Plutus ('riches'), since riches increase in time of peace. There is a marble copy of this work in Munich. The mother of these Horae was **Themis** ('law'), who often bore the epithet *Sōteira* ('savior'). She had sanctuaries at Athens, Delphi, Thebes, Olympia, and Troezen. She was represented as an austere, grave-looking woman, holding the cornucopia of blessing, and a balance as a symbol of justice, which weighs with exactness.

Aphrodite (Venus): Homer, Il. iii., *et passim;* Ovid, Met. iv. 171 *sq.*, Amor. i. 8, 42; Vergil, Aen. i. *passim;* Horace, Od. i. 4, 5; Hyginus, Fab. cxcvii.; Cowper, Translation from Milton i.:—
    Venus, preferring Paphian scenes no more.
Shak., The Tempest iv. 1, 93, Midsummer Night's Dream i. 1, 171, iii. 2, 61, Rape of Lucrece 9, Passionate Pilgrim *passim;* Chaucer, Knight's Tale 244.

Adonis: Ovid, Met. x. 532:—
    Caelo praefertur Adonis.
Vergil, Ecl. x. 18; Hyginus, Fab. ccxlviii.; Pope, Summer 61:—
    In woods bright Venus with Adonis stray'd;

Pope, Song by a Person of Quality iii.: —

> Thus the Cyprian Goddess weeping
> Mourn'd Adonis, darling Youth;
> Him the boar, in silence creeping,
> Gor'd with unrelenting tooth.

Cowper, Translation from Milton i.: —

> Adonis turned to Flora's favorite flower.

Shak., King Henry VI. pt. i. i. 6, 6, Venus and Adonis.
  Hermaphroditus: Ovid, Met. iv. 285 *sq*.
  Anchises: Homer, Il. v. 247, ii. 820: —

> Αἰνείας, τὸν ὑπ' Ἀγχίσῃ τέκε δῖ' Ἀφροδίτη.

Ovid, Trist. ii. 299; Vergil, Aen. i., *et passim*; Hyginus, Fab. xciv.
  Aeneas: Homer, Il. ii. *passim*; Vergil, Aen. i., *et passim*; Ovid, Met. xiii. 665; Shak., The Tempest ii. 1, 79, Midsummer Night's Dream i. 1, 173, King Henry VI. pt. ii. v. 2, 62, Julius Caesar i. 2, 112, Antony and Cleopatra iv. 14, 53.
  Eros (Cupid): Ovid, Amor. i. 1, *et passim*; Vergil, Aen. i. 658, 695; Byron, Childe Harold i. 9: —

> And where these are light Eros finds a fire.

Pope, Summer 13: —

> Ye cooling streams,
> Defence from Phoebus', not from Cupid's, beams.

Shak., The Tempest iv. 1, 90, Romeo and Juliet i. 4, 4, Merchant of Venice ii. 6, 38, Midsummer Night's Dream i. 1, 169, ii. 1, 161, iii. 2, 103; Chaucer, Knight's Tale 765.
  Musae: Homer, Il. ii. 484: —

> Μοῦσαι Ὀλύμπια δώματ' ἔχουσαι —
> ὑμεῖς γὰρ θεαί ἐστε, πάρεστέ τε ἴστε τε πάντα,
> ἡμεῖς δὲ κλέος οἶον ἀκούομεν οὐδέ τι ἴδμεν.

Ovid, Ars Amat. ii. 279: —

> Ipse licet venias Musis comitatus, Homere;

Amor. iii. 12, 17, Ibis 2; Vergil, Geor. ii. 475 *sq*.; Milton, Par. L. i. 6: —
  vii. 1: —

> Sing Heavenly Muse;

> Descend from Heaven, Urania, by that name
> If rightly thou art called, whose voice divine
> Following, above th' Olympian hill I soar,
> Above the flight of Pegasean wing.

Wordsworth, Ode (1814) v.: —

    And ye, Pierian Sisters, sprung from Jove
    And sage Mnemosyne.

Pope, Spring 11: —

    O let my Muse her slender reed inspire.

Shak., Sonnet xxxviii.; Spenser, F. Q. i. Pr. 2; Swift, Last Speech of Daniel Jackson: —

    There's nine, I see, the Muses, too, are nine.
    Who would refuse to die a death like mine!
    1. Thou first rung, Clio, celebrate my name;
    2. Euterp, in tragic numbers do the same.
    3. This rung, I see, Terpsichore's thy flute.
    4. Erato, sing me to the gods; ah, do't;
    5. Thalia, don't make me a comedy;
    6. Urania, raise me towards the starry sky;
    7. Calliope, to ballad strains descend,
    8. And Polyhymnia, tune them for your friend.
    9. So shall Melpomene mourn my fatal end.

Orpheus: Vergil, Geor. iv. 454; Ovid, Met. x. 3 *sq.*, xi. 22 *sq.*; Hyginus, Fab. xiv.; Pope, Summer 81: —

    But would you sing and rival Orpheus' strain,
    The wond'ring forests soon should dance again;
    The moving mountains hear the pow'rful call,
    And headlong streams hang list'ning in their fall!

Ode on St. Cecilia's Day 113: —

    Yet ev'n in death Eurydice he sung,
    Eurydice still trembled on his tongue,
    Eurydice the woods, Eurydice the floods,
    Eurydice the rocks, and hollow mountains rung;

Temple of Fame 83; Shak., Titus Andronicus ii. 4, 51: —

    As Cerberus at the Thracian poet's feet;

Two Gentlemen of Verona iii. 2, 78, Merchant of Venice v. 1, 79, King Henry VIII. iii. 1, 3, Rape of Lucrece 79.

2. The Divinities of War and Strife

116. The god that inflamed and stirred up war was called **Arēs** (Lat. *Mārs*). Originally he was the chief god of the warlike race of the Thracians, perhaps as a god of death dwelling in the depths of the earth, like the Zeus of the lower world (Hades-Pluto), and therefore also closely related to the earth's fruitfulness. Perhaps, however, he was a real heavenly Zeus in Thrace, and when imported into Greece was reduced to sonship, retaining the warlike attributes of his father as his own special characteristic.

At any rate, as might have been expected from the character of his early worshipers, he was developed into a wildly raging war god, and it was exclusively as such that he found entrance into Greece. Out of his ancient epithet, *Enyalios*, which seems to have referred to the wild war cry, was developed the idea that he had as a companion a destroying war goddess, Enyo (Lat. *Bellōna*). There were also associated with him Deimos ('terror'), and Phobos ('fright'), Eris the goddess of 'strife' (Lat. *Discordia*), and the **Kēres**, who were represented as dark-visaged women in bloody robes. The Keres were believed to cause death in battle, and are probably to be regarded as having been originally souls of the dead. Ares, however, represented only rude, violent warfare, so that he was constantly forced to give way before Athena and whoever chanced to be her protégés (*e.g.* Diomedes, in the Fifth Book of the Iliad).

117. In Greece Ares was looked upon as the son of Zeus and Hera, and in Thebes, the most important seat of his worship, Aphrodite was called his wife. The epic poets, however, harmonized two myths by making Aphrodite the wife of Hephaestus and at the same time the mistress of Ares. In Athens, where he was honored upon the Ἄρειος πάγος (Mars's Hill) as god of the atonement for murder, and of the tribunal that decided cases involving life and death, her place was taken by the dew nymph Aglauros. In art Ares was represented as a young and powerful man, in early times bearded and with full armor; later, beardless and usually clothed only with a helmet and a *chlamys*. His symbol was the spear. In worship he had as a further attribute an incendiary's torch, which was probably a symbol of the devastation produced by war.

Ares (Mars): Homer, Il. *passim;* Ovid, Amor. iii. 3, 27: —
> Nobis fatifero Mavors accingitur ense;

Met. iv. 170 *sq.;* Vergil, Geor. iv. 346: —
> Martisque dolos et dulcia furta;

Vergil, Aen. *passim;* Horace, Od. i. 6, 13; Hyginus, Fab. clix.; Dryden, Secular Masque 53: —
> Mars has look'd the sky to red;
> And Peace, the lazy God, is fled.

Shak., King Henry IV. pt. i. iv. 1, 116, King Henry V. Chorus i. 6, Antony and Cleopatra i. 1, 4, Hamlet iii. 4, 57; Chaucer, Knight's Tale 117, *et passim;* Spenser, F. Q. i. xi. 7.

Enyo (Bellona): Ovid, Met. v. 155, Fast. vi. 201; Vergil, Aen. viii. 703.

3. The Divinities of Destiny

118. When in human government order and justice, as opposed to the arbitrary will of the sovereign, gradually attained a commanding influence, it came to pass that, side by side with the gods of earlier times, who were represented entirely after the manner of human rulers tainted with passion, these ideas of order and justice gained an independent importance by being personified in the divinities of destiny. In Homer, as in the governments of his times, their position was still a vague one. The appointed lot, the **Moera** (more rarely found in the plural form, **Moerae**), or **Aisa**, is sometimes considered an expression of the will of Zeus; in other parts of the Homeric poems it already stands independently beside, or even above him, and he then, like the other gods, becomes merely the executor of its (or their) decrees. Therefore in Hesiod the Moerae are called sometimes daughters of night, at other times daughters of Zeus and Themis. They decide the fate of every man at his birth; and all the important events of his life, especially marriage and death, follow their decrees. From the time of Hesiod three Moerae were distinguished: Clotho ('spinner'), who spins the thread of life; Lachesis ('allotter'), the bestower of life's lot; Atropos ('the inevitable,' 'the unrelenting'), who sends death. Accordingly in art they carry as symbols a spindle and lots, sometimes also a scroll and a balance, as their mother Themis does. By the Romans they were identified with their Fates (*Parcae* or *Fāta*).

119. Nemesis, also, who appears personified first in Hesiod, represented originally the idea of the part measured out (*cf.* νέμω). She guards the preservation of the just measure; so her attributes are the cubit and the balance. Since she censures and punishes (νεμεσάω, νεμεσίζομαι) every violation of proper moderation, especially such as is occasioned by excessive self-confidence, she becomes also the angry requiter; and, as the one who subdues arrogance, she carries a bridle, yoke, and whip. But by the dropping of spittle into her bosom and the loosening of her garment it is especially indicated that she is the goddess who warns against presumptuousness; for it was customary to endeavor to shield oneself from the evil consequences of such presumption by these signs of self-abasement. As the goddess who will requite in the world to come she was adored at Athens at the feast of the *Nemeseia;* but she enjoyed real worship only at Rhamnus in Attica. (Concerning her identification with Leda see § 135.)

120. The latest of those personifications which gradually destroyed the old belief in the gods was **Tychē** ('the lucky accident,' Lat. *Fortūna*). She was indeed already personified by the earlier lyric poets, but did not enjoy any general adoration as a divine being until faith in the power of the older gods began to wane. In those times of unbelief she was first considered the dispenser of fruitfulness and wealth, as well as the disposer of human destiny, and the rescuer from the dangers of sea and war. Then in many cases she came to be regarded also as the protecting divinity of cities. As attributes she had the cornucopia and rudder, also a rolling wheel or a ball, to indicate the mutability of fortune.

121. The worship of such a goddess of chance, however, signifies properly nothing further than the denial of all actual divine power. So, after the destruction of the old positive faith in gods that were consciously and benignly guiding the world and human destiny, the Grecian world was preparing itself for the reception of the new doctrine of salvation emanating from Palestine. For though philosophy for a while tried to revivify the old dead forms by filling them with ethical ideas, it never could afford a really comforting, steadfast belief in a continued life after death, and in a justice that compensates for the defects of this earthly existence.

Parcae: Homer, Il. xx. 127; Hesiod, Theog. 217, 904; Old Verse: —

    Clotho colum retinet, Lachesis net, et Atropos secat.

Vergil, Ecl. iv. 46; Ovid, Trist. v. 3, 25; Hyginus, Fab. clxxi.; Shak., Pericles i. 2, 108: —

    Till the Destinies do cut his thread of life.

Tyche (Fortuna): Ovid, Trist. v. 8, 7; Vergil, Aen. viii. 334; Shak., King Henry V. iii. 6, 29.

C. THE GREEK HEROES

122. The warrior champions of the early ages were called 'heroes' (ἥρωες); but their worship as demigods does not surely date back beyond the ninth, or perhaps the eighth, century B.C., when it was recognized among the Aeolian tribes, particularly by the Boeotians, with whom also the worship of ancestors, a custom of very ancient origin, was always kept up. In almost every case the hero's grave, the customary place of sacrifice, was the central point of his worship.

In art they usually appear as warrior champions, often on horseback, or sitting on a throne, or reclining on a couch in their grave and feasting (if this is the correct interpretation of the 'funeral meal reliefs'), surrounded by their adorers. Therefore besides their armor and horse, and the serpent which has been shown above (§ 5) to be the representative of the soul, a cup became their usual attribute.

1. THEBAN LEGENDS

123. Cadmus, the founder of Cadmea, to which he himself as its eponymous hero owes his name, was the legendary ancestor of the noble tribe which settled on the site of the citadel of Thebes. At a neighboring spring dwelt a dragon descended from Ares. This Cadmus slew, and from the sowing of its teeth in the ground sprang up the brazen Sparti ('sown men'), *i.e.* the indigenous inhabitants of Thebes. After most of these had killed each other in the fratricidal war cunningly incited by Cadmus, he founded Cadmea with the help of the five survivors, *i.e.* the ancestors of the noble families of Thebes. Then he married Harmonia ('harmony'), who was the daughter of the Boeotian national god Ares and of Aphrodite,—a myth that probably refers to the beginnings of political organization. Of their children, Ino and Semele were especially conspicuous. At last Cadmus and his wife, like other heroes, assumed the form of serpents, but both were removed by Zeus to Elysium. A later legend, emanating especially from Delphi, transfers the home of Cadmus to Phoenicia, and makes him a son of Agenor, king of Tyre. According to this version, Agenor sent Cadmus forth in company with his brothers, the national heroes, Phoenix, Cilix, and Thasus, to search for his sister Europa, who had been carried off by Zeus; and in his wandering he reached Boeotia and founded Thebes.

124. Antiopē ('the one looking toward you') was a Boeotian-Corinthian, perhaps closely akin to Selene. On the mountain Cithaeron she bore the Zeus-begotten twins Amphion and Zethus, who are probably, like the Laconian Dioscuri, to be regarded as divinities of light. When afterwards, being cruelly tormented by **Dircē**, the jealous wife of her uncle Lycus, she fled to Cithaeron, she met her sons, who had been reared by a shepherd. They did not recognize her. But on the occasion of a Dionysus-festival she was again caught by Dirce and in punishment for her flight was about to be dragged to death, bound to the horns of a bull. Just then the sons learned from their foster father the secret of their origin, rescued their mother, and visited the cruel punishment with which she had been menaced upon Dirce herself, who after her death was changed into a spring near Thebes. The fastening of Dirce to the bull was represented in the second century B.C. by Apollonius and Tauriscus of Tralles in the marble group commonly known as "the Farnese bull," which is now in Naples.

The twin brothers obtained the sovereignty in Thebes, and surrounded the lower city with a wall in which were seven gates. The stones dragged along by the powerful Zethus piled themselves up in layers regularly of themselves by the magic of Amphion's playing on the lyre, — a legend that was probably intended to glorify the regulating power of music, in which the same symmetry prevails as in architecture.

125. Amphion wedded the daughter of Tantalus, **Niobē**, who had inherited from her father conscious pride. When she had borne six sons and six daughters, she boasted that she was richer than Leto, who had but two children. Apollo and Artemis, however, revenged the insult offered their mother, by killing the children of Niobe, who in grief at their loss was turned into stone and removed to Mount Sipylus in Lydia; whereupon Amphion put himself to death.

A representation of the killing of the children of Niobe was executed by Scopas or Praxiteles, probably for the city of Seleucia in Cilicia. This group was later brought to Rome. We are acquainted with most of its figures through Roman copies (the most complete group of which is in Florence).

Cadmus: Ovid, Met. iii. 1 *sq*., Trist. iv. 3, 67; Hyginus, Fab. vi.; Pope, Thebais i. 8: —
> And Cadmus searching round the spacious seas?
> How with the serpent's teeth he sow'd the soil.

Chaucer, Knight's Tale 688.
  Agenor: Ovid, Met. iii. 51; Hyginus, Fab. clxxviii.
  Amphion: Vergil, Ecl. ii. 24: —
> Amphion Dircaeus.

Ovid, Met. vi. 271; Horace, Ars Poet. 394; Pope, The Temple of Fame 85: —
> Amphion there the loud creating lyre
> Strikes, and beholds a sudden Thebes aspire!

Thebais i. 12.
  Dirce: Hyginus, Fab. vii.
  Niobe: Homer, Il. xxiv. 602; Ovid, Met. vi. 148 *sq*.; Hyginus, Fab. ix., x., xi., cxlv.

2. Legends of Argos, Mycenae, and Tiryns

126. As has been learned from excavations, the district of Argos had intimate relations with Egypt and Asia even as early as the flourishing period of the city Mycenae, a period which perhaps extended from 1450 to 1250 B.C. The same relations appear also in the myths of this region; the story of Io and Danaüs suggests an alliance with Egypt; that of Perseus and the Pelopidae, one with Asia.

Iō, the daughter of the river god Inachus, was beloved by Zeus; therefore the jealous Hera transformed her into a heifer, and caused her to be guarded by the many-eyed, 'all-seeing' (*Panoptos*) **Argus** in the vicinity of Mycenae, until, at the command of Zeus, he was put to sleep and killed by Hermes, who perhaps thus won the epithet *Argeiphontēs* ('Argus-slayer'?). Upon this Io was pursued over sea and land by a gadfly sent by Hera; but finally in Euboea or Egypt she regained her human form, and bore Epaphus, the father of Danaüs and Aegyptus.

127. Danaüs, the representative of the Danaï dwelling in Argolis in the times of Homer, migrated to Greece with his daughters, the Danaïdes, according to the legend, and became king of Argos. The fifty sons of Aegyptus followed them and courted them, but, with the exception of Lynceus, whom his wife Hypermnestra spared, were all murdered by them on their wedding night at the command of Danaüs, — a figurative description of the rivers of Argos (sons of the Aegyptus stream) becoming quite dry in summer through the drying up of the springs (Danaïdes). In punishment for this murder the Danaïdes were compelled in the lower world to draw water in a perforated vessel, an idea that is closely connected with their significance as fountain nymphs.

128. A descendant of Lynceus was Acrisius, king of Argos. Through an oracle he learned that he was to be killed by a grandson. Therefore he concealed his daughter **Danaē** in a brazen tower and kept her strictly guarded. Zeus, however, penetrated to her in the form of golden rain, and she became the mother of **Perseus**. Acrisius then shut both mother and child up in a chest and threw them into the sea. Simonides of Ceos, with delicate poetic appreciation of their fearful peril, describes the situation as follows: —

> When, in the carven chest,
> The winds that blew and waves in wild unrest
> Smote her with fear, she, not with cheeks unwet,
> Her arms of love round Perseus set,
>   And said: O child, what grief is mine!
> But thou dost slumber, and thy baby breast
> Is sunk in rest,
> Here in the cheerless brass-bound bark,
> Tossed amid starless night and pitchy dark.

Nor dost thou heed the scudding brine
Of waves that wash above thy curls so deep,
Nor the shrill winds that sweep, —
Lapped in thy purple robe's embrace,
Fair little face !
But if this dread were dreadful too to thee,
Then wouldst thou lend thy listening ear to me ;
Therefore I cry, — Sleep, babe, and sea be still,
And slumber our unmeasured ill !
Oh, may some change of fate, sire Zeus, from thee
Descend, our woes to end !
But if this prayer, too overbold, offend
Thy justice, yet be merciful to me !

(Translated by J. A. Symonds.)

Finally they reached the island of Seriphus, where they were brought to land by the fisherman Dictys. When Perseus had grown up, Polydectes, the ruler of the island, who was a suitor of Danaë, and found the son in his way, inveigled the young man into a promise to go and bring the head of the Gorgon Medusa. By the assistance of Hermes and Athena, Perseus succeeded in cutting off the head of the monster while she was asleep, — that head the very sight of which petrified every one who gazed upon it; but he escaped from the pursuing sisters of Medusa only by borrowing the helmet of Hades, which rendered him invisible. In Ethiopia (Rhodes?) he rescued the daughter of Cepheus, **Andromeda**, who had been bound fast to a rock on the shore as a propitiatory offering to a sea monster which had been sent by Poseidon. Then after changing all his enemies into stone by showing them the Gorgon head, and after fulfilling the oracle by killing his grandfather inadvertently by a throw of the *discus*, he ruled in Tiryns with his wife Andromeda, and from there built Mycenae.

129. A more recent family, yet one that even before the Dorian migration was powerful in Argos and a large part of the surrounding Peloponnesus, was that of **Tantalus,** who, at the same time, dwelt upon Mount Sipylus in Asia Minor. He is a mythological figure similar to Atlas, the mountain god, who bears up the heavens; and his name, too, seems to mean "bearer." To him, as the son of Zeus, the gods vouchsafed their confidential intercourse, but by his gross covetousness and his presumption he forfeited their favor. Therefore he was cast down to the lower world, and there stood, tormented by hunger and thirst, in the midst of water, under a tree loaded with fruits; for water and tree alike receded as often as he stretched out his hand toward them. According to another legend a rock hung over his head constantly threatening to fall upon him.

130. The children of Tantalus were Niobe and **Pelops,** after whom the Peloponnesus ('island of Pelops') is said to have been named. Pelops sued for the hand of Hippodamia ('tamer of horses'), the daughter of king Oenomaüs of Elis, and won her as a wager in a chariot race with her father, who lost the race, and perished, through the treachery of his charioteer Myrtilus. The preparations for this contest were represented in the eastern pediment of the temple of Zeus at Olympia.

Atreus, the son of Pelops, was ruler of Mycenae after the death of Eurystheus. According to the older legend, which is followed in the Iliad, his brother Thyestes inherited the kingdom from him in a lawful manner. On the other hand, the later epic poets and the tragic writers entangle the descendants of Tantalus in a series of terrible crimes. According to them Thyestes robbed his brother Atreus of his sovereignty and his wife, and brought about the death of his son. Atreus, however, after regaining the royal power, revenged himself by slaying the sons of Thyestes and setting their flesh as food before their unwitting father. For this, Atreus, in turn, was afterwards murdered by a son of Thyestes, Aegisthus, whom Atreus had treated as his own son and brought up as such.

131. Agamemnōn and **Menelāus**, the real sons of Atreus, in due time dispossessed Aegisthus of the kingdom. The former became king of Mycenae, and the latter of Lacedaemon. Paris, the handsome son of Priam of Troia ('Troy'), eloped with Helen, the wife of Menelaüs. In order to avenge this outrage, the two Atridae ('sons of Atreus') collected a mighty Grecian army, whose leadership Agamemnon assumed. When the hosts had assembled at Aulis, contrary winds prevented their setting sail, because their leader had offended the goddess Artemis. According to the decision of the seer Calchas, the goddess could be propitiated only by the sacrifice of Agamemnon's daughter, Iphigenia. Thereupon the king sent a messenger to his wife Clytaemnestra at Mycenae, to tell her that she must send her daughter to the camp to be wedded to Achilles. When, however, in response to this deceptive summons, Iphigenia arrived, and was dragged to the altar to be offered, Artemis interposed and carried her off to Tauris (the Crimean peninsula), and a hind was found standing at the altar in place of the maiden. Agamemnon, now, with many other heroes, proceeded against Troy. Meanwhile Aegisthus seduced Clytaemnestra, who was angry at her husband on account of the attempted sacrifice of Iphigenia; and the guilty pair finally murdered the king when he returned ten years later, after the conquest of Troy. In Laconia, Chaeronea, and Clazomenae, however, Agamemnon was worshiped in later times as a Zeus of the lower world, under the name of Zeus *Agamemnōn* (*cf. Z. Basileus*), in the form of a scepter, the symbol of dominion.

At the murder of her father, the elder daughter of Agamemnon, Electra, rescued her youthful brother **Orestēs**, and took him to Strophius, king of Phocis, with whose son Pylades he formed a close friendship. When grown up to young manhood he hastened back to Mycenae to take vengeance on his father's two murderers. In the *Electra* of Sophocles, and still more in Euripides's play of the same name, Electra, whom her mother has so wronged, herself goads her brother on to the dreadful murder, when he hesitates at the sight of his mother. Clytaemnestra falls first, pierced by her son's sword; afterwards, Aegisthus also. But Orestes has scarcely shed his mother's blood before the Erinyes start in his pursuit. Restless and miserable, he wanders about until at the bidding of the Delphic oracle he goes to Tauris, for the purpose of taking the image of Artemis which was there to Greece. Being caught in the attempt to carry this off, he is about to be slain as an offering to the goddess. But there he finds in the temple his sister Iphigenia as a priestess; and by her assistance he escapes, carrying with him his sister and the image of the goddess. Pylades, who has accompanied him everywhere, now marries Electra, while Orestes himself weds the beautiful Hermione, the daughter of Menelaüs and Helen.

Argus: Ovid, Amor. iii. 4, 19: —
Centum fronte oculos, centum cervice gerebat;
Met. i. 624 *sq.*, ii. 533: —
Tam nuper pictis caeso pavonibus Argo.
Vergil, Aen. vii. 791; Pope, Thebais i. 355: —
And there deluded Argus slept, and bled.
Spenser, F. Q. i. iv. 17.
Epaphus: Ovid, Met. i. 748; Hyginus, Fab. cxlix., cl.
Danaüs: Ovid, Her. viii. 24; Hyginus, Fab. clxviii., clxx.
Danaë: Ovid, Met. iv. 611; Vergil, Aen. vii. 410; Hyginus, Fab. lxiii.; Tennyson, The Princess vii. 167: —
Now lies the Earth all Danaë to the stars
And all thy heart lies open unto me.
Perseus: Homer, Il. xiv. 319; Ovid, Met. iv. 610 *sq.*, v. 16 *sq.*, "Sappho" 35; Hyginus, Fab. lxiii., lxiv.; Pope, Sappho to Phaon 41: —
An Ethiopian dame
Inspired young Perseus with a generous flame;
Temple of Fame 80: —
And Perseus dreadful with Minerva's shield.
Cepheus: Ovid, Met. iv. 737, v. 12 *sq.*; Hyginus, Fab. lxiv.
Andromeda: Ovid, Met. iv. 757 *sq.*; Hyginus, Fab. lxiv.
Tantalus: Homer, Od. xi. 582; Hyginus, Fab. lxxxii.; Pope, Thebais i. 345: —
The guilty realms of Tantalus shall bleed.
Atlas: Ovid, Her. ix. 18: —
Hercule supposito sidera fulsit Atlans;
Met. iv. 632 *sq.*, Fast. v. 180; Vergil, Aen. iv. 481: —
Ubi maximus Atlas
Axem humero torquet stellis ardentibus aptum.
Milton, Par. L. ii. 306: —
With Atlantean shoulders fit to bear
The weight of mightiest monarchies.
Cowper, Translation from Milton, To his Father: —
And Atlas stands unconscious of his load.
Pope, Thebais i. 138: —
Affrighted Atlas, on the distant shore,
Trembled, and shook the heav'ns and gods he bore.
Shak., King Henry VI. pt. iii. v. 1, 36.

Pelops: Ovid, Met. vi. 403 *sq.;* Vergil, Geor. iii. 7; Hyginus, Fab. lxxxiii., lxxxvi.–lxxxviii.
Hippodamia (Daughter of Oenomaüs): Ovid, Her. viii. 70; Hyginus, Fab. lxxxiv.
Oenomaüs: Ovid, Ibis 365 *sq.;* Hyginus, Fab. lxxxiv.
Thyestes: Ovid, Ars Amat. i. 327; Hyginus, Fab. lxxxvi., lxxxviii.
Aegisthus: Ovid, Rem. Amor. 161; Hyginus, Fab. lxxxvii.
Agamemnon: Homer, Il. *passim;* Aeschylus, Agamemnon; Sophocles, Electra; Euripides, Orestes; Ovid, Met. xv. 855; Horace, Od. iv. 9, 25; Hyginus, Fab. xcvii.
Menelaüs: Homer, Il. *passim;* Ovid, Ars Amat. ii. 359; Vergil, Aen. vi. 525; Hyginus, Fab. cxviii.; Shak., King Henry VI. pt. iii. ii. 2, 147; Troilus and Cressida Prol. 9.
Paris: Homer, Il. *passim;* Ovid, Epis. v., xv., xvi.; Vergil, Ecl. ii. 61, Aen. i. 27; Hyginus, Fab. xci., xcii.
Helen: Homer, Il. *passim*, Od. iv. *passim;* Euripides, Helen; Vergil, Aen. vii. 364; Hyginus, Fab. lxxix; Shak., King Henry VI. pt. iii. ii. 2, 146, Troilus and Cressida Prol. 9.
Iphigenia: Euripides, Iphigenia at Tauris, Iphigenia at Aulis; Ovid, Met. xii. 31, Ex Pont. iii. ii. 62; Hyginus, Fab. xcviii., cxx.
Orestes: Aeschylus, Choëphori; Euripides, Orestes, Iphigenia; Ovid, Ex Pont. iii. ii. 69 *sq.*, Her. viii.; Hyginus, Fab. cxix.
Hermione: Homer, Od. iv. 14; Ovid, Her. viii.

3. Corinthian Legends

132. The relations were intimate between Argos and Corinth, which, in consequence of its situation, developed very early into an important commercial town, and was especially influenced by Phoenicia. As early as the Iliad we find mention of the crafty, covetous **Sisyphus**, ruler of Ephyra, *i.e.* the Acrocorinth, who later sank down to the level of a mere arithmetician and intriguer, the type and copy of the average Corinthian merchant. Because he had offended Zeus he was condemned in the lower world to keep eternally rolling a rock up a steep hillside, though it always rolled down again as soon as it reached the summit. Since at other times Sisyphus is also characterized as an old sea god, this punishment may be considered a symbol of the waves of the sea ceaselessly rolling the stones to and fro on the shore.

133. His grandson **Bellerophontēs** (or, in a shortened form, **Bellerophōn**) possessed the winged horse Pegasus. With the help of this horse, having been sent to Lycia, he killed the frightful Chimaera ('goat'), a monster composed of a fire-breathing she-goat, a lion, and a serpent. Originally this was an imaginative representation of the thundercloud sending forth the ragged, roaring, and serpentine lightning; but later it probably symbolized also the volcanic phenomena of Lycia. Bellerophon fought successfully with the mountainous race of the Solymi, the neighbors of the Ethiopians and Lycians (*i.e.* of the inhabitants of the land of light), and also with the Amazons. At last he attempted on his thunder-horse to enter heaven itself, but was flung down and perished miserably,—a legend no doubt representing the lightning darting down from heaven to earth. In Corinth, as well as in Lycia, he received adoration as a divine being. Bellerophon, as is evidenced by his relation to Pegasus, the embodiment of the thundercloud, and by his killing the monster of the thunderstorm, was a figure closely related to the lightning hero Perseus, who was indigenous to the neighboring Argos.

Sisyphus: Homer, Il. vi. 153, Od. xi. 593 *sq.*; Ovid, Met. iv. 460, Fast. iv. 175; Hyginus, Fab. lx.; Pope, Ode on St. Cecilia's Day 66:—

> Thy stone, O Sisyphus, stands still.

Spenser, F. Q. i. v. 35.

Bellerophon: Homer, Il. vi. 155 *sq.*; Hyginus, Fab. lvii.
Pegasus: Ovid, Met. iv. 786; Hyginus, Fab. lvii.; Spenser, F. Q. i. ix. 21; Shak., King Henry V. iii. 7, 11.
Chimaera: Homer, Il. vi. 179; Ovid, Met. ix. 647: —
> Quoque Chimaera jugo mediis in partibus ignem,
> Pectus et ora leae, caudam serpentis habebat.

Vergil, Aen. vi. 288; Hyginus, Fab. lvii.

4. Laconian Legends

134. Before the Dorian migration the most important place in Laconia was Amyclae, situated south of Sparta, and one of the chief seats of the worship of Apollo. Here, or in Sparta, ruled Tyndareüs and his wife **Lēda**. The latter became by Zeus, who was enthroned upon the neighboring mountain Taÿgetus, the mother of the Dioscuri ('sons of Zeus'), Pollux (Gk. *Polydeukēs*) and Castor. Afterwards, when Zeus in the form of a swan had approached her, she bore Helen also. To Tyndareüs she bore Clytaemnestra; and in the later version Castor also, who was a mortal, was regarded as his son.

135. The **Dioscūrī**, who were perhaps ancient divinities of light, had their chief abode in Laconia, Messenia, and Argos, but after a while their worship spread over the whole Grecian world, so that they were everywhere invoked as rescuers in danger (*Sōtēres*), or as rulers (*Anakes*), particularly in battle or in storms at sea. Sometimes their sister Helen was worshiped as a protecting goddess with them. She may be considered a moon goddess, and was in later times called the daughter of avenging Nemesis only on account of her fatal significance for Troy and the Greek people. Both Dioscuri were believed to ride upon white horses; and, besides being a master of horsemanship, Pollux was regarded as a powerful boxer. After the death of Castor, who was slain by the Messenian hero Idas, Pollux obtained from Zeus permission for himself and his brother to spend the time together forever, by living one day in the lower world and the next on Olympus.

In art the Dioscuri appear usually as youthful riders, clad only in the chlamys, and armed with the lance. As heroes, the serpent was their attribute; but later the pointed, egg-shaped hat ($\pi\hat{\iota}\lambda$ος), or the addition of two stars, characterized them.

Leda: Homer, Od. xi. 298; Ovid, Her. xvi. 55, Met. vi. 109; Hyginus, Fab. lxxvii.; Keats, Endymion i. 157: —
> Wild thyme, and valley lilies whiter still
> Than Leda's love, and cresses from the rill.

Dioscuri (Pollux and Castor): Ovid, Amor. iii. 2, 54: —
> Pollucem pugiles, Castora placet eques;

Fast. v. 709 *sq.;* Hyginus, Fab. lxxx.; Macaulay, Battle of Lake Regillus 2.

Idas: Homer, Il. ix. 558; Ovid, Fast. v. 700 *sq.*

5. Hercules

136. Herculēs (Gk. *Hēraklēs*) was the son of Zeus and Alcmene ('strength'), the wife of king Amphitryon of Thebes, and thus was a descendant of Perseus. His names are as various as his functions. In his youth, *i.e.* in Thebes, where the story of his youth is laid, he was called also Alcaeus ('the strong'), from which is derived his epithet *Alcīdēs*. His principal name, which is probably of Argive origin, it has not yet been possible to explain with certainty. The second part, *culēs* (κλης), belongs, like the fuller form κλειτός, to κλέος ('fame'); but whether or not the first part is connected with *Hērā̆*, ("Hρα), the protecting goddess of Argos, who imposed upon him his labors, cannot be positively decided. While he was worshiped especially by the Boeotians, Dorians, and Thessalians (as, indeed, it was with the Boeotians that all hero worship in its full development appeared first), yet from the earliest times in Athens, Marathon, and Leontini, he enjoyed divine honors as *Alexikakos* ('defender from evil'), and *Kallinīkos* ('glorious victor'). In later times he was regarded as the chief representative of the wrestling art and therefore also as the founder of the Olympian games; and his statue appeared everywhere in the gymnasiums and adjacent baths, so that he became by such association the god of all warm baths and other healing waters or springs. On account of his clearing the highways of enemies, he appears also as the god that escorts travelers (*Hēgemonios*). He is often attended by his protectress Athena, more rarely also by Hermes and Apollo.

137. He was hated by Hera, just as were all the sons of Zeus begotten from other wives. Therefore, since Zeus had decreed the dominion over Argos to the next descendant of Perseus who should be born, Hera delayed the birth of Hercules until his cousin Eurystheus had seen the light of day in Mycenae, and had thus become ruler of Argos, and liege lord of Hercules. Evidently, however, Tiryns was regarded as the birthplace of Hercules; for the distant Thebes, though spoken of in the Iliad as his home, never can have stood in such a dependent relation to Mycenae as would be implied by the legend just mentioned.

While yet in his cradle Hercules strangled two **serpents** which Hera had dispatched against him. After he had slain with the lyre his teacher **Linus**, who had chastised him, Amphitryon sent him to tend flocks upon Mount

Cithaeron, where he killed a powerful lion. When his father had fallen in battle against the Orchomenians, Creon, the last of the Sparti, became king of Thebes, and to Hercules was given his daughter **Megara** as a wife. In a fit of madness, which Hera decreed upon him, he killed his three children with bow and arrows. On his recovery he was compelled in expiation of his crime to enter the service of **Eurystheus**, who laid upon him a series of difficult labors, the order of which varies in different versions of the myth. The collection of legends describing these labors forms the connecting link between the Theban-Boeotian and the Argive-Dorian Hercules myths. The latter of these two series of myths seems to embrace the labors in their oldest form.

138. According to this version Hercules had his abode in Tiryns, south of Mycenae, to which, indeed, the story of his birth points. (1) He fought at Tiryns, as he had done on Cithaeron, with a powerful **lion**, which lived on Mount Apesas, between Nemea and Mycenae. After this he wore the skin of this lion, flung over the upper part of his body, as a characteristic dress. (2) Accompanied by his friend and charioteer, **Iolaüs**, he went against the **Hydrā**, a nine-headed water serpent in the marshy springs of Lerna, south of Argos. In place of every one of the monster's heads that was struck off two new ones grew, until Iolaüs set the neighboring woods on fire and burned out the wounds (*i.e.* dried up the springs). The last immortal head Hercules covered with a block of stone. Then he moistened the tips of his arrows with the venom of the monster.

139. (3) From Mount Erymanthus in Arcadia, from whose snow-covered summit a wild mountain stream of the same name rushes down, a **wild boar** (a symbol of this stream) was laying waste the fields of Psophis. Hercules pursued him up into the glaciers, and brought him in chains to Eurystheus, who in terror hid in a cask. On Mount Pholoë, which is near Erymanthus, he lodged with the Centaur **Pholus**, who was named after the mountain and was a counterpart of Chiron, who dwelt on the Thessalian Pelion. As Hercules was being there regaled with the wine which belonged to all the Centaurs in common, he fell into a quarrel with them, and finally killed most of them with his arrows. Pholus and Chiron perished also by carelessly wounding themselves with some of the arrows. Then, after Hercules, still operating in Arcadia, had (4) caught the **hind** of Cerynea and (5) driven out the **storm birds** whose nests were on the lake of Stymphalus, birds that shot out their feathers like arrows, his native land of Argolis was insured against all dangers.

140. The scenes of the following expeditions were farther away. (6) Upon an Elean local legend rests the story of the cleansing of the stables of king **Augeās** ('the beaming one'), of Elis. Though three thousand cattle had been kept there, the cleansing must be completed in a single day. This feat, according to the tradition, Hercules accomplished by conducting the river **Mēnios** ('moon river') through the place. But upon a metope of the temple of Olympian Zeus, the only extant representation in art of this adventure, he is represented as using a long broom. Augeas promised Hercules for his labor a tenth part of his herds, but did not keep his word; wherefore he and all his champions were afterwards slain by Hercules after a stubborn resistance.

141. Perhaps there is some connection between this last legend and that (10) (usually put in the tenth place in the series) of the robbery of the cattle of the giant **Gēryonēs** ('roarer'), who likewise ruled in the far west on the island Erythea ('red land'). In order to ride over Oceanus, Hercules compelled Helios to lend him his sun skiff; then he killed the three-bodied giant with his arrows. When returning, he overpowered the fire-breathing giant **Cācus** on the site of the future city of Rome, who had stolen from him and hidden in a cave a part of the cattle of Geryones which he had carried off. In Sicily, moreover, he defeated **Eryx**, a mighty boxer and wrestler, the representative of the mountain of the same name.

(7) The seventh adventure, the binding of the **Cretan bull**, and (9) the ninth, the fight with the **Amazons**, the girdle of whose queen, Hippolyte, he is said to have demanded on a commission of Eurystheus, are perhaps borrowed from the legends of Theseus, who accomplished similar acts; but since Hercules's battle with the Amazons appeared in works of art somewhat earlier than that of Theseus, the reverse process, namely that of a transfer from Hercules to Theseus, is not impossible. (8) As his eighth task, Hercules received the command to fetch the horses of the Thracian king **Diomēdēs**. Diomedes dwelt in the far north, and his horses were fed on human flesh. This task was accomplished after throwing the cruel king before his own horses.

142. His last two adventures are closely connected with each other, both representing how Hercules, at the end of his life, laboriously obtained immortality by his journeys into the lower world and into the garden of the gods. These ideas, to be sure, were afterwards, with the union of the Argive and the Thessalian-Oetaean legends, supplanted by the myth that he destroyed himself by fire. (11) On the way to the garden of the **Hesperides** ('western'), who guarded the golden apples of rejuvenation, and dwelt where the edge of the western sky is gilded by the setting sun, he throttled the giant **Antaeus**, lifting him up from the Earth, his mother, who was constantly supplying him with new strength. Then he slew king **Būsīris** in Egypt, who cruelly sacrificed all strangers cast upon the coast of his country. In the name Busiris certainly lurks that of the Egyptian god Osiris. Finally, after liberating **Promētheus**, who had been chained on Caucasus by Zeus, he came to Atlas, who bore the heavens upon his shoulders (as every mountain apparently does). Hercules begged him to pluck three apples from the tree of the Hesperides. Meanwhile he himself took Atlas's place in bearing up the heavens, or, in his own person went into the garden of the gods and slew the dragon that guarded the tree.

143. (12) The bringing up of the hellhound **Cerberus** from the lower world was put last, on the ground of its being the most difficult labor. Evidently it had been forgotten that the fetching of the apples that bestow eternal youth out of the land imagined to be in the extreme west properly signified the reception of Hercules among the gods. This latter thought was certainly represented in the later idea (which likewise probably belongs to the Argive legend) of the marriage of Hercules with **Hēbē** ('bloom of youth'). She was the daughter and counterpart of Hera (who by this time had been appeased), while the

Italian legend unites its Hercules with Juno herself. Hercules went down into the lower world at the promontory Taenarum, freed Theseus from his imprisonment, chained Cerberus, and came up with them at Troezen or Hermione.

Another, perhaps an older, form of the same legend is apparently to be seen in the story, mentioned as early as the Iliad, of the expedition of Hercules against Pylus ('gate' of the lower world), during which he wounded with three-pointed arrows his inveterate enemy Hera, and also **Hādēs**, the ruler of the lower world. After the completion of the labors imposed upon him by Eurystheus, the servitude of Hercules came to an end. The application of the number twelve to his labors seems, however, not to have been definitely made until about 480 B.C.

144. The third principal group of the Hercules myths is formed by the expeditions located in Thessaly and on Oeta. To this group originally belonged also his sacking Oechalia, and his servitude to Omphale. Hercules sued for the hand of Iole, the daughter of the mighty archer Eurytus, who ruled in Thessalian Oechalia. But though he defeated her father in an archery contest, she was refused him. A short time thereafter, in revenge, he hurled her brother **Īphitus** down from a precipice, although he was staying as the friend and guest of Hercules; and later he also took the city, and carried Iole with him as a captive. To be absolved from this bloodguiltiness, he went to Delphi; but Apollo delayed his answer. Then Hercules seized the holy tripod, to carry it away; the strife thus kindled was stopped by the interposition of a lightning flash from Zeus. Hercules was now told by the oracle that he could be ransomed from his guilt only by a three years' servitude.

145. Hermes therefore sold him to **Omphalē**, who was in later times commonly regarded as queen of the Lydians and as ancestress of the Lydian kings; probably, however, she is only the eponymous heroine of a city Omphalium, which is believed to have existed in early times on the border between Thessaly and Epirus. For in her service he scourged the **Itonians**, *i.e.*, of course, the inhabitants of the Thessalian Itonus, where he also fought with the mighty **Cycnus**. He punished likewise the sly thieves, whose home was near Thermopylae, the **Cercōpes**, and also **Syleus** ('robber') on Pelion. But Lamios (or Lamus), the son of Hercules and Omphale, is merely the eponym of the city Lamia, situated not far north of Trachis. Perhaps it was not till after the home of the legend was transferred to Lydia that the poetic addition to the story was made that Hercules clothed himself as a maidservant and worked with the distaff, while Omphale adorned herself with his lion's skin and his club.

146. Directly connected with these legends, and, as their field of action is in the neighboring Aetolia, probably allied in origin, is Hercules's wooing of **Dēianīra** ('husband-destroyer'). She was the daughter of king Oeneus in Calydon, a country abounding in vines, where, to gain possession of her, Hercules (probably as the representative of civilization) was forced to fight with the wild river god Acheloüs. The latter appears sometimes as a natural river, again as a bull, and still again as a man with a bull's head. Not until Hercules breaks off one of his horns does he acknowledge himself conquered, and offers, in order to recover it, to give in exchange the horn of the she-goat Amalthea, *i.e.* the horn of plenty, from which issues a stream of nourishment and blessing. Yet this horn properly belongs to Hercules himself as the dispenser of fruitfulness, in which capacity he was much worshiped, especially in the country. A counterpart of the battle with the river god is furnished by the wrestling match (usually introduced in connection with the Hesperides adventure) with **Halios Gerōn**, the old man of the sea, who afterwards is called Nereus or Triton.

147. On his journey back to Trachis Hercules killed the Centaur **Nessus** (this being a counterpart of his battle with the Centaurs on Mount Pholoë), who attempted to offer violence to Deïanira while carrying her on his back across the ford of the river Evenus. The dying Centaur advised her to catch up and take with her the blood streaming from his wound, saying that it would act as a love charm. Some time later, hearing that after the capture of Oechalia Hercules had made the beautiful Iole his prisoner, Deïanira rubbed this blood upon a garment and sent it by Lichas to her husband on his way home. Hercules had scarcely put it on before the poison of Nessus pierced through his body. In fury at his torment he flung Lichas into the sea, but could not remove the garment, which clung to his limbs and tore the flesh off with it. Deïanira killed herself in pure desperation; but Hercules charged his son **Hyllus** to marry Iole, mounted a funeral pyre erected on the summit of Mount Oeta, and by the gift of his bow and arrows persuaded **Poeās**, the father of Philoctetes, or, according to another account, Philoctetes himself, to apply the torch. Amid thunder and lightning he ascended to heaven, being thus purified by fire, and became one of the gods. According to a passage in the Iliad there existed in some places the belief that Hercules, in obedience to a decree of fate, and in consequence of the wrath of Hera, actually died and was staying in the lower world. The same view really prevails in the Odyssey also; but in the latter poem the idea of a later elaborator, who was striving to reconcile the myths, caused only the ghost of Hercules to appear.

148. Taking him all in all, Hercules in the later period was the ideal type of a valiant, noble Dorian man; and in many parts of these legends he may be the exact representative of the Dorian race (which reverenced him especially) in its migrations and battles. Yet since many other features of his mythical history cause him to be recognized as an old sun god, we may perhaps assume that, like the gods of the Iliad, he first appeared in battle fighting for his worshipers, and then gradually became, from the protecting deity, the representative of the race, and at the same time the type of the Dorian warrior.

149. The oldest image with the form of which we are well acquainted connected with the worship of Hercules is that of Erythrae, where he, like other heroes, acted as a god of healing by means of oracular dreams. According to coins upon which this image is imitated, Hercules was there represented as standing upon a boat, without the lion's skin, a club in his right hand, which was raised; in his left, a spear (or stick?). In other very old representations also he is nude; later he appears wearing complete armor and a short tight-fitting cloak. At length, somewhere about 600 B.C., the type with the lion's skin, beginning in Cyprus and Rhodes, came to predominate, probably under the influence of Phoenician models, in imitation of **Melkart**, the sun god and king of Tyre, with whom Hercules was later identified in many respects. His hair and beard are usually closely cut; it is very rare that he appears without a beard in works of the older period. After the beginning of the fourth century B.C. he is again regularly represented entirely nude; he carries the lion's skin on his left arm, his club in his right hand. Praxiteles gives him a deeply sorrowful expression; Lysippus, the attitude of motion, especially at the hips. To the latter sculptor is doubtless to be traced the general type of the weary Hercules resting; the special form of this, however, preserved in the so-called 'Farnese Hercules' in Naples, was of later origin. In the representations of his deeds, Hercules usually in earlier works, as in the story of the Iliad, carries a bow as his weapon; more rarely, and indeed principally in works of Ionian origin, the club; in those originating in the Peloponnesus, the sword, which, according to the Odyssey, he carried in addition to his bow.

Hercules: Homer, Od. xi. 601 *sq.*; Sophocles, Trachiniae; Euripides, Herakles; Ovid, Met. ix. 256 *sq.*, Her. ix.; Vergil, Aen. vi. 801 *sq.*; Horace, Ep. xvii. 31; Hyginus, Fab. xxx., xxxvi., clxii.; Shak., Midsummer Night's Dream iv. 1, 117, Love's Labour's Lost i. 2, 69, v. 2, 592; Pope, The Temple of Fame 81: —

> There great Alcides, stooping with his toil,
> Rests on his club and holds th' Hesperian spoil.

Milton, Par. L. ii. 542.

Amphitryon: Ovid, Her. ix. 44; Hyginus, Fab. **xxix**.

Creon: Homer, Od. xi. 269; Sophocles, Antigone; Chaucer, Knight's Tale 80 *sq*.

Hydra: Ovid, Met. ix. 69 *sq.*; Vergil, Aen. vi. 287; Horace, Od. iv. 4, 61; Hyginus, Fab. **xxx**.; Pope, Thebais i. 502: —

> The foaming Lerna swells above its bounds,
> And spreads its ancient poisons o'er the grounds.

Geryones: Ovid, Her. ix. 92; Vergil, Aen. vii. 662, viii. 202.
Hippolyte: Apollod. ii. 5, 9; Diodor. Sic. iv. 16; Vergil, Aen. xi. 661; Chaucer, Knight's Tale 10.
Hesperides: Ovid, Met. iv. 637 *sq.;* Vergil, Aen. iv. 483 *sq.;* Milton, Par. L. iv. 249 : —
> Others whose fruit burnisht with golden rind
> Hung amiable, Hesperian fables true.

Antaeus: Ovid, Met. ix. 183; Hyginus, Fab. xxxi.
Omphale: Ovid, Fast. ii. 305 *sq.;* Hyginus, Fab. xxxii.
Philoctetes: Sophocles, Philoctetes; Ovid, Met. xiii. 329; Hyginus, Fab. cii.

6. Theseus

150. The Ionians, a trading people, who worshiped Poseidon, had their principal homes in Euboea, the eastern coast of Attica, and Argolis, and on the islands that formed the connecting link with the Ionian colonies on the coast of Asia Minor. They forced their way into Athens from the east and south; therefore **Iōn**, their mythological ancestor, is really foreign to Athens, and only through his mother, **Creūsa**, daughter of Erechtheus, is connected with the native ruling family of Cecrops. Of a more primitive character than this unworshiped ancestor of the Ionian race is **Thēseus**, who, being especially an Ionian, was developed, like Hercules among the Dorians, into the ideal Ionian hero. His home, properly, was Troezen in Argolis, a city which must probably be regarded as a very ancient center of the unification of the Ionian race; for the temple of Poseidon that served as the federate sanctuary of an old Ionian Amphictyonic league (sacrificial confederacy) was situated on the island Calauria, which is off the coast of Troezen.

151. Sometimes Poseidon himself, and sometimes king Aegeus of Athens, who is only a representative of this god, and owes his mythical existence to a mere epithet (*cf.* αἶγες = 'springing ones' = waves), was regarded as the father of Theseus. His mother was Aethra ('the bright, happy one'), daughter of Pittheus, king of Troezen. Before Aegeus left her on his return to Athens, he hid his sword and sandals under a heavy stone, with the charge that his son should be sent to him as soon as he could lift it. When grown to young manhood, Theseus, taking the sword and sandals for a countersign, so to speak, passed over the isthmus in search of his father. On the way he slew several robbers: the club-brandishing Periphetes; the fir-bender, Sinis; Sciron, who dwelt on a steep pass by the sea; the wrestler Cercyon; and the giant Damastes, who tortured strangers on a bed, and was therefore called Polypemon ('hurter'), or Procrustes ('stretcher'). He also overcame the wild sow of Cromyon.

152. Meanwhile Aegeus had married the enchantress Medea. When Theseus arrived in Athens, she wanted to poison him; but he was spared, his father recognizing him by the sword that he had brought. He now smote the gigantic Pallas and his mighty sons, who rose against Aegeus; then he bound the Cretan bull, which had been released by Hercules and had ranged from Mycenae to Marathon. This adventure, however, is really only a later and secondary form of his contest with the bull-headed monster called the Minotaur, the story of which is usually told as follows: —

153. Androgeos, a son of king Minos of Crete, had been slain by the Athenians. To atone for this murder they were compelled to send to Gnosus, every year for nine years, seven boys and seven girls to be devoured by the **Minotaur**, who was shut up in a labyrinth. Theseus voluntarily went with these victims. On his arrival in Crete, Minos's daughter Ariadne fell in love with him and gave him a ball of yarn, with the advice to fasten the end of it at the entrance of the labyrinth when he went in, that by following the thread he might retrace his way out of the countless interlacing paths. The plan was successful; and after slaying the Minotaur he sailed away with his companions, whom he had rescued. With them he secretly took Ariadne herself, and landed with them all either on the neighboring island of Dia, or on Naxos. Here Ariadne was left behind, and according to one form of the legend, probably the older one, was killed by Artemis, because she had been already previously united in wedlock with Dionysus, and had preferred a mortal to him. According to the version that prevailed later, it was here that, after Theseus had secretly abandoned her, she was wedded to Dionysus, whose worship was prominent on Naxos.

154. On his departure from Athens Theseus had promised his father that in case the undertaking against the Minotaur was successful he would substitute for the black mourning sail of his vessel a white one. But he forgot his promise, and Aegeus on the approach of the ship cast himself down either from a cliff of the Acropolis, or into the sea, which derived its name 'Aegean' from him. In later times he was reverenced in Athens as a hero.

Theseus, to commemorate his prosperous return, established the autumn festival of **Pyanepsia** ('bean festival'), and that of the grape gathering, *Oschophoria* ('carrying around of vine branches'). As ruler he consolidated twelve individual communities into the united state of

Athens at the southern base of the ancient Acropolis, an event that lived on in the memory of the people through the celebration of the old *Synoikiā* ('uniting of habitations'), and probably gave him his name Theseus = 'the founder.' (*Cf.* θήσειν and τιθέναι.)

155. Like Bellerophon, Hercules, and Achilles, Theseus also fought against the **Amazons**, either as a comrade of Hercules, or on the occasion of an invasion made by the Amazons into Attica. At the same time he won the love of Antiope or Hippolyte, who had been conquered by him (*cf.* Achilles and Penthesilea), married her, and begot Hippolytus ('unyoker of horses'), a hero worshiped in Troezen and Sparta, who probably was originally a sun god. Afterwards Phaedra ('the shining one,' a moon goddess related to Aphrodite), whom Theseus had married after the death of the Amazon, became enamored of her chaste stepson Hippolytus, and, when her passion was not reciprocated by him, brought about his death by falsely accusing him of making improper proposals to her.

156. At Marathon, which belonged to the old Ionian tetrapolis ('four states') of Attica and was the scene of his struggle with the bull, Theseus met the Thessalian **Pirithoüs** ('daring attempter'), king of the Lapithae, and formed a close friendship with him. Then, as we read in the Iliad (though the passage is much disputed), on the occasion of his friend's marriage to Hippodamia, or Deïdamia, Theseus fought beside him against the wild **Centaurs** of Mount Pelion, as in their drunkenness they laid wanton hands on the women. This scene frequently appears in the art of the first half of the fifth century B.C., notably in the metopes of the Parthenon, and in the group designed by Alcamenes in the western pediment of the Temple of Zeus at Olympia. But in the earlier works, from the seventh century B.C. on, Hercules is the regular opponent of the Centaurs. Together with Pirithoüs, Theseus then carried off the youthful **Helen** from Sparta, and brought her to the mountain stronghold Aphidnae in northern Attica, from which she was afterwards released by her brothers, the Dioscuri. Meanwhile Theseus (probably, according to the older idea, at Hermione) went down into the lower world with his friend to steal **Persephonē** for him. Both of them grew fast to a rock at the entrance, but Theseus was afterwards released by Hercules.

157. During the absence of Theseus, Menestheus, who in the Iliad is leader of the Athenians, had usurped the power at Athens. Theseus was therefore compelled, soon after his return from the lower world, to leave the city again. He went to the island Scyros, and was there treacherously cast into the sea by king Lycomedes. Later, however, Demophoön and Acamas, sons of Phaedra, gained the dominion in Athens. The bones of Theseus, which, it was claimed, had been miraculously discovered, were brought to Athens from Scyros in the year 468 B.C., and interred in a newly erected sanctuary between the gymnasium of Ptolemaeus and the Anakeion. His real worship at Athens began after the opening of the fifth century B.C., when the Ionian democracy came into power.

158. In art Theseus was represented perhaps even as early as the eighth or the seventh century B.C. in battle with the Minotaur, or standing near Ariadne. In works of the sixth century the contests with the bull and the

Amazons appear, as well as the rape of Helen. None of the other adventures is to be found until the fifth century B.C. In the oldest representations his weapon is the sword, and in dress and bodily frame he is still undistinguished from other heroes. Later, in imitation of the Hercules type, he usually carries a club and often a beast's skin; but he is distinguished by the headdress of youth and by being more slender.

Doubtless Theseus is a personality originally related to the Boeotian-Argive-Thessalian (Dorian) Hercules; but his form has been perfected to correspond to the Ionian ideal of a hero. Like Hercules, he has many characteristics of an old sun god; it being especially common that such divinities, as in this case, were considered the founders of communities of a race or a city.

Cecrops: Ovid, Met. ii. 555; Hyginus, Fab. xlviii.

Theseus: Ovid, Met. vii. 404 *sq.*, Fast. iii. 473; Hyginus, Fab. xxxviii., xlii., xliii.; Chaucer, Knight's Tale 2, *et passim*.

Aethra: Ovid, Her. x. 131; Hyginus, Fab. xxxvii.

Medea: Euripides, Medea; Ovid, Met. vii. 11 *sq.*, Her. xii., xvi. 229; Hyginus, Fab. xxv., xxvi., xxvii.; Shak., Merchant of Venice v. 1, 13; King Henry VI. pt. ii. v. 2, 59; Chaucer, Knight's Tale 1086.

Hippolytus: Euripides, Hippolytus; Ovid, Fast. iii. 265; Vergil, Aen. vii. 761 *sq.*; Hyginus, Fab. xlvii.; Spenser, F. Q. i. v. 39.

Pirithoüs: Homer, Il. i. 263, xiv. 317; Ovid, Met. xii. 218.

Hippodamia (daughter of Atrax): Ovid, Met. xii. 210 *sq.*

CYCLES OF MYTHS

1. MELEAGER AND THE CALYDONIAN HUNT

159. Meleager, the son of Oeneus, of Calydon, and Althaea, was a mighty hunter. With many companions he laid low a terrible wild boar sent by Artemis, which was ravaging the fields. But in a quarrel that arose out of the award of the prize of victory he slew a brother of his mother. She besought the gods of the lower world to avenge the murder on her son. Soon afterwards he fell in battle. The post-Homeric poets add that the Moerae had informed his mother soon after his birth that her son would live only until a piece of wood then glowing on the hearth should be consumed by the fire; whereupon she quickly quenched it and saved it; but after the murder of her brother she caused the death of her son by burning the stick.

160. Another later addition to the myth was that the shy Arcadian-Boeotian huntress **Atalanta**, who is closely akin to Artemis, the hunting goddess, was associated with Meleager. In consequence of his love for her he promised her the head of the boar as a prize of honor, because she had been the first to wound the animal; thus he fell into the quarrel with his uncle and met his death, as told above. But Atalanta would have for her husband only one that could defeat her in a foot race, the condition being that all defeated suitors should be put to death. Milanion (according to another version, Hippomenes) received from Aphrodite three golden apples, which at her advice he flung before Atalanta during the race. While she was picking them up he reached the goal before her, and so she was compelled to become his wife.

Althaea: Ovid, Met. viii. 446 *sq.*; Hyginus, Fab. clxxi.
Meleager: Homer, Il. ix. 543 *sq.*; Ovid, Met. viii. 270 *sq.*; Hyginus, Fab. clxxiv.; Chaucer, Knight's Tale 1213.
Atalanta: Ovid, Met. x. 565 *sq.*, Ars Amat. iii. 775; Hyginus, Fab. clxxxv.; Chaucer, Knight's Tale 1212.

2. The Argonauts

161. The myth of the Argonauts unites the legends of the Thessalian city Iolcus and the Boeotian Orchomenus, both of which were inhabited by the old race of the Minyae, with those of Corinth, which from the earliest times had been closely connected with the far east by navigation; and this union is so complete, probably under the influence of the Ionian epic poets, that the real basis of the myth can no longer be ascertained with certainty. Iolcus was the home of **Jāsōn**, the leader of the Argonauts. He was the son of Aeson, but was under the guardianship of his uncle Pelias, and, like Achilles, Aesculapius, and Hercules, was brought up on the neighboring Pelion by the Centaur Chiron and instructed in medical science. During his absence Pelias, as Pindar sings in his fourth Pythian 'ode of victory,' had been given the following oracle: "That in every way he should keep careful guard against the man of one sandal, whenever from the steep pastures to the sunny land of renowned Iolcus he shall come, be he stranger or native" (vv. 75-78).

As Jason on his return homeward had lost a shoe in crossing the river Anaurus, Pelias feared that by him he should be robbed of his power, and therefore sent him on an expedition to bring the golden fleece from Aea, the land of Aeetes, in the hope that the youth would perish in the attempt. Jason collected a large band of heroes, built the first large ship, the Argo ('the swift'), under the protection of Hera overcame all the dangers threatening him, and after his return ruled in Iolcus, wedded to Medea, the daughter of Aeetes.

162. For Medea persuaded the daughters of Pelias to kill their own father, and promised to bring him to life again and to renew his youth, but did not fulfill her word. According to the later version of the legend, which combines its individual features in a confused manner, she then fled with Jason before Pelias's son Acastus to Corinth, while magnificent funeral games were celebrated in honor of the murdered man. **Alcēstis** was the only daughter of Pelias that took no part in the murder of her father. She afterwards voluntarily died for her husband **Admētus,** the king of Pherae, since according to the will of the Moerae he could be saved by the sacrificial death of another. She was then brought back from the realm of death by Hercules.

163. The myth of the **golden fleece** seems to have developed principally in Orchomenus. King Athamas, who of course is closely related to the Athamantian plains near Halos in the Thessalian Phthiotis, had from Nephele ('cloud') the children Phrixus and Helle. When his second wife Ino instigated him to sacrifice Phrixus to Zeus *Laphystios,* to remove the unfruitfulness of the land, Nephele carried off her children through the air upon a golden-fleeced ram furnished her by Hermes. On the way Helle fell into the arm of the sea named after her (*Hellespont*), while Phrixus successfully reached Aea, the land of the light of sunrise and sunset, which was located sometimes in the east and sometimes in the west. He there offered the ram in his stead to Zeus *Laphystios,* and hung up its golden fleece in the grove of Ares, where it was guarded by a dragon. In this part of the myth a process of nature is symbolized, the carrying away of a rain cloud gilded by the sun, which is also at other times thought of as a shaggy pelt, being thus picturesquely expressed. On the other hand, the story of the offering and rescue of Phrixus may have originated in the worship of Zeus *Laphystios*, where for the sacrifice of a human being that of a ram may have been afterwards substituted, a process such as may lie at the foundation of the legend of Iphigenia. The story relating to Helle was perhaps added only to explain the name Hellespont.

164. The **Mēdēa** myth and the further development of the expedition of the Argonauts is of Corinthian origin; for their goal is designated as the eastern land Colchis, well known to the Corinthian navigators. Moreover, Aeetes, the son of Helios and Persa, while he is a personality that surely originated in an epithet of the sun god, is generally considered to have been a ruler of Corinth, on whose citadel, Ephyra or Acrocorinth, Helios himself had one of the chief seats of his worship, and afterwards to have emigrated to Colchis. When Jason demanded from him the golden fleece, Aeetes declared himself ready to comply if he would first yoke two fire-breathing bulls with brazen feet and with them plow the field of Ares. Medea, who was inflamed with love for the stranger, protected him from the effect of the fire by a magic ointment, and helped him to overpower the dragon which was guarding the fleece.

165. Then with the Argonauts she embarked in the ship, at the same time carrying off her young brother **Apsyrtus.** When pursued by Aeetes, she killed the boy and flung his limbs one by one into the sea, that her father might be retarded by the search for them. After an adventurous voyage, which later forms of the legend, with the widening of geographical knowledge toward the north and west, constantly extended further, they reached Corinth (or returned to Iolcus), where they obtained the kingdom. When Jason afterwards divorced Medea to wed the daughter of king Creon, Medea killed Creon and all his daughters by means of a magic poisoned garment. Then, after murdering both of her own children, she fled to Athens in a chariot drawn by dragons, where she married Aegeus. In consequence of her unsuccessful murderous attack upon Theseus she returned to her home in Asia.

Medea is the mythical prototype of all witches, who were similarly charged with murdering children; but at the same time she is so closely related to the moon goddesses Hecate and Hera that she must herself be regarded as a moon heroine. Jason, however, may be a figure resembling the Boeotian Cadmus, and may have received his name from Ἰαωλκός, Iolcus.

166. To this, the simplest form of the myth of the Argonauts, was by degrees added a whole series of local legends and sailors' tales, and an ever-increasing number of heroes were mentioned as having joined in the expedition. It was said that at Chalcedon, on the Bosporus, Pollux had defeated in a boxing contest the giant Amycus ('tearer'), who had prevented the navigators from gaining access to a spring. On the other side of the Bosporus the Argonauts met the blind king **Phineus**, who was tormented by Harpies. As soon as he sat down to eat, the Harpies came along and seized or befouled the food. They were therefore pursued by Zetes and Calaïs, the sons of Boreas, and driven away forever (*cf.* the Stymphalides). To express his gratitude for this service, Phineus told his rescuers how to avoid the further dangers of the voyage, particularly how to pass successfully the rocks of the **Symplēgades** ('striking together'), which crushed ships between them. These rocks, which can still be distinguished at the entrance of the Bosporus, were said to be floating islands, which were afterwards fixed in their present position. In the adventure in Colchis itself the sowing of the dragon's teeth by Cadmus (*cf.* § 123) was transferred to Jason.

Argo; Argonauts: Pindar, Pyth. iv.; Vergil, Ecl. iv. 34: —
> Vehat Argo | delectos heroas.

Ovid, Amor. ii. 11, 6, Her. xii. 9; Hyginus, Fab. xiv.–xxi.; Milton, Par. L. ii. 1017: —
> And more endanger'd, than when Argo pass'd
> Through Bosporus betwixt the justling rocks.

Pope, Ode on St. Cecilia's Day 40: —
> While Argo saw her kindred trees
> Descend from Pelion to the main.

Apollon. Rhod., Argonautica.

Jason: Apollod. i. 9, 16; Ovid, Met. vii. 5 *sq.*, Epis. xvi. 229; Hyginus, Fab. xxii., xxiii., xxiv.

Aeson: Ovid, Met. vii. 162 *sq.;* Pope, Dunciad iv. 121: —
> As erst Medea (cruel so to save!)
> A new edition of old Aeson gave.

Cowper, Translation from Milton ii. 10: —
> Aeson-like to know a second prime.

Pelias: Ovid, Met. vii. 298 *sq.;* Hyginus, Fab. xii.

Aeetes: Ovid, Met. vii. 9; Hyginus, Fab. xxii.

Alcestis: Euripides, Alcestis; Hyginus, Fab. l., li.

Admetus: Euripides, Alcestis; Ovid, Ex Pont. iii. 1, 106, Trist. v. 14, 37; Hyginus, Fab. l., li.

Phrixus; Helle: Ovid, Epis. xvii. 141 *sq.*, Fast. iii. 852 *sq.;* Hyginus, Fab. i., ii., iii.

Apsyrtus: Ovid, Trist. iii. 9, 6; Hyginus, Fab. xxiii.

Phineus: Ovid, Met. v. 8 *sq.;* Hyginus, Fab. xix.

3. THE THEBAN CYCLE

167. In the myths that are brought together in the Theban cycle there appears this pervading thought, that man is not able, either by wisdom or by strength, to carry out his own plans in opposition to the will and predestination of the gods. On the contrary, the very prudence that strives to render of none effect such decrees of the gods as have been announced by oracles or other signs helps to fulfill the divine will. This appears most simply in the oldest part of the cycle, the expedition of the Seven against Thebes, described in the *Thēbais*. A later counterpart is the expedition of the Epigoni ('the after-born'); and the same thought is brought out in a more complicated manner in the Oedipus myth, which contains the preliminary history of this contest, and which Cinaethon of Sparta (?) had used in his *Oidipodeia*. Finally, the *Alkmaiōnis*, a sequel to the story of the Epigoni, and a work belonging to the end of the sixth century B.C., described the tremendous punishments inflicted by the gods in avenging the murder of relatives. In the extant *Thēbais* of the Roman poet Statius the principal ideas of all these lost epics are combined. But this group of myths is still further perfected from the purely moral point of view in the Attic tragedy, and is represented in the following extant plays: the 'Seven against Thebes' of Aeschylus, the 'Oedipus Tyrannus,' 'Oedipus at Colonus,' and 'Antigone' of Sophocles, the 'Phoenissae' of Euripides.

168. According to a divine decree Laïus, the son of Labdacus, was to be the last of the family of Cadmus who should be king of Thebes. Therefore he received from the oracle at Delphi the utterance: "If thou beget a son, he will murder thee and marry his own mother." So when his wife Iocaste, whom the epic poets called Epicaste, the sister of Creon, the last of the Sparti,

K

bore him a son, Laïus pierced his feet, bound them together, and caused him to be exposed on the neighboring mountain Cithaeron, that thus by killing his child he might render impossible the fulfillment of the oracle. But the child was discovered by a shepherd, brought to king Polybus at Sicyon or Corinth, and by him named **Oedipūs** ('swollen-footed'). When the boy had grown up, being taunted about his parentage, he asked the oracle at Delphi to reveal to him his real origin, but received as answer only the ominous response, that he must become guilty of incest with his mother, and kill his father. In order to make the threat ineffective, he did not return to Corinth; yet even before he had gone far from Delphi he met his father Laïus at a fork in the road, and being provoked by him, killed him without being aware who he was.

169. Meanwhile Thebes had been visited with a severe scourge. The **Sphinx** ('throttler'), a monster, the upper part of whose body was a winged maiden, and the lower part that of a lion (probably, like the "nightmare," a creature born of "such stuff as dreams are made of," though afterwards it was thoroughly confused with the similarly formed Egyptian-Babylonian symbol of power and swiftness), dwelt upon a mountain in the vicinity of the city and submitted to passers-by this riddle: "What walks in the morning on four legs, at midday on two, and at evening on three?" She had killed all that had not guessed it, among them, according to an older legend, Haemon, the son of Creon, who after the death of his brother-in-law Laïus ruled in Thebes. Creon now offered as a reward to anybody freeing them from this scourge the hand of the queen and the sovereignty of Thebes.

Oedipus correctly solved the riddle as referring to man, who creeps on all fours when a child, walks upright in middle life, and uses the support of a staff in old age.

170. Oedipus accordingly became king in his native city, and, at the same time, his mother's husband. According to the epic poets the gods soon made this crime known, probably through the seer Tiresias, as the later form of the legend states. Epicaste killed herself and Oedipus blinded himself. Afterwards, by a second wife, Eurygania, he had the sons Eteocles and Polynices, and the two daughters Antigone and Ismene. The tragic poets mention no second marriage of Oedipus, but rather treat all these as the children of Iocaste herself.

Later, on account of some trifling fault, Oedipus brought upon his sons the curse that they should divide the inheritance by the edge of the sword. He himself then died in Thebes, or, according to the Attic version, in banishment in the sanctuary of the Semnai at Colonus, near Athens, under the protection of Theseus.

171. Eteoclēs and **Polynīcēs** fell into a quarrel in dividing the inheritance and the power; whereupon the latter fled to Adrastus, king of Argos and Sicyon, and became his son-in-law. He then equipped an expedition against his brother, of which Adrastus undertook the command. Polynices was further supported by his brother-in-law, the Aetolian Tydeus, a fiery son of Oeneus of Calydon; also by Hippomedon and Parthenopaeus, the brothers of Adrastus; by the mighty Capaneus; and lastly by the courageous seer Amphiaraüs, brother-in-law of Adrastus. Amphiaraüs, indeed, foresaw that they should almost all perish in the expedition, but was nevertheless induced to take part in it by his wife Eriphyle, who had been bribed by means of a beautiful necklace, which, however, brought ruin to its possessor. Therefore he charged his son Alcmaeon ('the strong') that as soon as he grew up he should take revenge upon her for his death.

172. In spite of omens, which predicted all sorts of evil, the Seven, trusting in their own power, advanced against Thebes and assaulted the seven gates of the city. Capaneus had already scaled the walls, when a bolt from the hand of Zeus dashed him down again. The two brothers Eteocles and Polynices killed each other in single combat, yet the fight continued to rage with fearful fury. Tydeus, even in the throes of death, lacerated with his teeth the head of his fallen antagonist and sipped the brains out of the gaping skull. Amphiaraüs was buried alive with his chariot close by Thebes in a chasm in the ground, which Zeus opened in front of him by a thunderbolt. Here he ruled as a spirit giving out oracles by means of dreams. He was greatly revered also in other places, especially at Oropus in the district of Psaphis; but originally he was none other than Hades himself, invoked under the name of 'the besought on every side.'

173. Adrastus, saved by his swift war horse Arion, was the only one of the seven to escape. The Thebans were persuaded by him, or, according to the Attic version of the story, were compelled by Theseus, to deliver up the fallen for burial. Aeschylus and Sophocles add at this point the story of Antigone's fate. According to them Polynices was to remain unburied as an enemy to his native land. But his sister Antigone, contrary to this command, dragged him upon the funeral pyre of Eteocles, or at least covered him with earth. She was seized by the appointed watchers and punished by death for this deed, which was nevertheless called for by sisterly love and divine law.

174. Ten years later the sons of the fallen heroes (the Epigoni), now led by the favor of the gods, marched against Thebes, took it and demolished it, and set over it as ruler Thersander, the son of Polynices. The whole expedition, however, is described by the later poets as a counterpart of the former one. Alcmaeon, the leader of the host, before setting out fulfilled the command of his father by murdering his mother to avenge him. But although Apollo himself had given his consent to this, the murderer, like Orestes, was pursued by the Erinyes until after long wanderings he finally obtained rest through a new oracular response.

Iocaste: Homer, Od. xi. 271 *sq.*; Sophocles, Antigone 861, Oedipus Rex; Hyginus, Fab. lxvi., lxvii.

Oedipus: Homer, Od. xi. 271; Sophocles, Oedipus Rex, Oedipus at Colonus, Antigone; Hyginus, Fab. lxvi.; Pope, Thebais i. 21:—

> At Oedipus—from his disasters trace
> The long confusions of his guilty race;

Thebais i. 69:—

> Now wretched Oedipus, depriv'd of sight
> Leads a long death in everlasting night;

Thebais i. 336:—

> His sons with scorn their eyeless father view.

Eteocles: Hyginus, Fab. lxvii.; Sophocles, Antigone; Aeschylus, Seven against Thebes 182 *sq.*; Pope, Thebais i. 219.

Polynices: Sophocles, Oedipus at Colonus, Antigone; Hyginus, Fab. lxvii.-lxxii.

Antigone: Aeschylus, Seven against Thebes 862; Sophocles, Antigone, Oedipus Rex, Oedipus at Colonus; Hyginus, Fab. lxxii.

Amphiaraüs: Aeschylus, Seven against Thebes 569 *sq.*; Ovid, Ex Pont. iii. 1, 52:—

> Notus humo mersis Amphiaraüs equis.

Hyginus, Fab. lxxiii.

4. THE ACHAIAN-TROJAN CYCLE

175. A part of the Achaians once emigrated from Thessaly to Argolis. Some of them were forced by the Dorians into Achaia, and afterwards settled lower Italy. Others went to Asia Minor, and there in company with the Achaians of Thessaly, who migrated thither at the same time, obtained by conquest new homes in the vicinity of Troy, which was then lying in ruins. It was probably the effort to explain the origin of these ruins, which went back to a prehistoric period, that caused the migrating Grecian tribes to connect them with old myths of their own people. Taking their idea from the conquest of this same land, which they had just made an accomplished fact, they fancied the destruction of Ilios-Troia to have been the result of a campaign of their own ancestors.

176. This whole legendary subject-matter was treated in the following independent epics, which group themselves round the Iliad and the Odyssey: (1) The *Cypria*, by a Cyprian poet, perhaps Stasinus; a work originating after the completion of the interpolated additions to the Iliad. (2) The Iliad of Homer, who may have lived about 850 B.C. (3) The *Aithiopis* of Arctinus of Miletus, written perhaps about 750 B.C. (4) The 'Little Iliad' of the Lesbian Lesches, of the first half of the seventh century B.C. (5) The 'Destruction of Ilios' ('Ιλίου πέρσις), also by Arctinus. (6) The 'Homeward Voyages' (Νόστοι), by Agias of Troezen, later than Arctinus and the Odyssey. (7) The Odyssey, to be dated somewhere about 775 B.C. (8) The *Tēlegoniā*, by Eugammon of Cyrene, about 570 B.C.

177. Of the foregoing, aside from fragments and meagre excerpts, only the Iliad and the Odyssey are extant.

These were recognized by the ancients themselves as the most noble gems in the crown of epic poetry. Both of them were in earlier times ascribed to the poetic genius of one man, Homer, who surpassed all others; but the great dissimilarity that appears in the social relations and the religious conceptions described forces us to conclude that the two poems must be attributed to different authors, at least in their present form. Seven cities claimed Homer as their citizen. Smyrna, the first mentioned of these, seems to have the best right to the claim, for it appears from the Iliad itself that the poet probably came from the region near the mouth of the river Hermus. In its original form the poem described only the momentous quarrel between Achilles and Agamemnon. But into this oldest epic, which formed the foundation of the whole Trojan chain of myths and contains the germ of all other poems on the subject, there were certainly introduced at a later period many kinds of interpolations, and at the same time the whole was probably revised; yet even in its present form the dramatic plot which lies at its foundation is so plainly visible that there can be no doubt of its conscious formation by one individual poet.

178. The keynote of the drama of the **Iliad** is struck by a description of the plague brought upon the Grecian host by Apollo, on account of an injury done to his priest Chryses in the tenth year of the siege of Troy. Just as in the progress of the chief plot the haughtiness of the commander in chief, Agamemnon, is to blame for the grievous losses and defeats of the Greeks, so here he has caused this wrath of Apollo by refusing to listen to the request of one of his priests for the restoration of a daughter who has been carried away among the spoils of war. At this point comes in the dramatic 'motive': **Achillēs** (Gk. *Achilleus*), the noblest champion in the Grecian camp, in the name of the army, which has been victorious up to this time, demands from Agamemnon that he surrender this maiden Chryseïs. The plot deepens as follows: Agamemnon indeed grants the request, but in compensation for his own loss, takes away from Achilles the girl Briseïs, who has been given to him as a present by the army. Thereupon Achilles in anger withdraws from battle, and at his request his mother Thetis prays Zeus, the disposer of battle, to grant victory to the Trojans until her son shall have received full satisfaction.

179. In Books ii.-vii. comes the first climax, in a subsidiary plot. First Agamemnon tries to bring about an end of the war, without Achilles, by a single combat between Paris, who carried off Helen, and her rightful husband Menelaüs. Paris, being vanquished, is rescued by Aphrodite, but the treaty is immediately broken by a treacherous shot of the Trojan Pandarus. Now the Achaians advance, and Diomedes, the son of Tydeus and ruler of Argos, who is under the special protection of Athena, and Ajax, the son of Telamon of Salamis, next to Achilles the most valiant of the Grecian heroes, distinguish themselves in single combats. As Agamemnon already fancies that he has nearly won the victory over Troy, and at the same time over his rival Achilles, Zeus, out of regard for his promise made to Thetis, forbids the gods to take any further part in the struggle. Consequently the Greeks are driven back into their camp, whereupon the second climax begins, and this time in the main plot (Books viii.-xii.).

180. In order not to be forced to give way to Achilles, Agamemnon seriously proposes to give up the siege altogether. But Diomedes and the aged Nestor, who rules the Messenian and Triphylian Pylus, and who surpasses all the other chieftains in wisdom and eloquence, hinder him by their opposition. Therefore the Greeks attempt once more to conquer in open battle, but suffer a complete defeat, and Agamemnon himself is wounded, like most of the other champions.

The chief climax of the action, and the apparent approach of victory for the hero of the drama, *i.e.* Achilles, are marked by the battle round the ships (Books xiii.–xv.). Hector, the most valiant son of king Priam of Troy, and Apollo force their way into the Grecian camp and set fire to the ships, at which the destruction of the whole host seems almost inevitable. Then in the direst necessity comes a change in affairs, caused by the wavering of Achilles himself. Half renouncing his decision, he sends to the assistance of the hard-pressed fighters his friend **Patroclus**, whom he allows to put on his own armor and to take command of his Myrmidons. They drive the enemy out of the camp; but as Patroclus, against his friend's command, pursues the Trojans, he is killed by Hector (Book xvi.).

181. At this point begins the decline of the action (Books xvii.–xxi.). The final 'motive' of dramatic interest is the surrender of Briseïs to Achilles and the humiliation of Agamemnon. Yet even now Achilles's victory is only apparent, as he himself well understands. For he, the champion, has invited against himself the charge of arrogance, since, on account of the merely personal injury done him by Agamemnon, he has too long inactively viewed the destruction of his people. This fault of his causes the death of Patroclus, and with it the catastrophe (Book xxii.). After obtaining through his mother new weapons from Hephaestus, Achilles kills Hector, although he knows that he himself must inevitably die shortly after laying low this enemy, and Hector himself, when mortally wounded, reminds him of the certainty that such a fate will befall him. The action comes to an end with the funerals of Patroclus and Hector and the lament of Achilles over the loss of his friend. In his lament he is preparing himself for his own death, which follows so immediately that, so far as Homer is concerned, it follows only behind the scenes.

182. It cannot at present be decided whether we may attribute to Homer some sort of an original sketch, or rough draft of the **Odyssey**, which served as a model for all the poets describing the return home of the Trojan heroes; but at any rate this poem, as well as the Iliad, was laid out according to a plan exhibiting a unity that has been marred only by later interpolations. Among these interpolations is, together with the larger part of the last book, the whole 'Telemachy' (Books i.–iv.), in which the journey of Telemachus to Pylus and Laconia is described. To get information concerning the whereabouts of his father, who has now been away nearly twenty years, he goes to the aged Nestor, and then to Menelaüs. Each tells him of his own return home and of that of other heroes. From Menelaüs he learns also that his father is a prisoner on the island of the nymph Calypso in the far west. But before Telemachus gets back to Ithaca, his father himself has already arrived there. His journey therefore has no influence on the course of events.

183. The old *Nostos* ('homeward journey'), like the Iliad — and this speaks strongly for the identity of their authors — described only the last year of the wanderings, *i.e.* the catastrophe proper, while the previous events were set forth by a narrative put into the mouth of Odysseus. During his wanderings on the return from Troy, **Odysseus** (Lat. *Ulixēs,* Eng. Ulysses), the ruler of the little island of Ithaca, has lost his companions and ships. Though consumed with longing for his home, he lives for seven years on the island Ogygia with the nymph **Calypsō** ('the concealer'), who tries to create in him a permanent attachment for herself. But with longing equal to his own his faithful wife **Pēnelopē** awaits his return in Ithaca, although wooed by numerous haughty suitors. Finally, induced by Athena's request, Zeus commands the nymph to release Odysseus. On a raft he approaches the island of the **Phaeāces**. But here Poseidon dashes his craft to pieces, and only by the help of the goddess Ino-Leucothea is he able to swim to the shore.

184. Nausicaa, the daughter of king Alcinoüs, gives him clothing and directs him to her father's palace. At the king's table he himself tells of his previous adventures. He had lost many of his comrades in battle with the brave **Cicones.** The others had tasted the sweet fruit of the Lotus in the land of the **Lōtophagī** ('Lotus-eaters'), and he had been compelled to drag them to the ships by main force, since eating it had made them forget their native land and their friends. Then the voyagers had come into the cave of the one-eyed Cyclops **Polyphēmus,** who devoured several of them, but finally in a drunken sleep was blinded by Odysseus. Since Polyphemus was a son of Poseidon, that god was now angry at Odysseus and his companions. Next they came to **Aeolus**, the ruler of the winds, who, being graciously disposed towards them, shut up all contrary winds in a bag; and so they might have reached home safely if the comrades of Odysseus had not secretly opened the bag.

185. Then all the ships except the one on which Odysseus himself was sailing were wrecked by the gigantic **Laestrȳgones**. With the one remaining ship he reached the island of the enchantress **Circē**, who at first metamorphosed a part of the crew into swine; but on being threatened by Odysseus, she restored them to their human form, and they were then all gladly received by her. On her advice Odysseus proceeded to the entrance of the lower world, to ask the shade of the seer **Tiresiās** about the way homewards. Past the islands of the bird-formed **Sirēnes** ('Sirens'), who charm men by their singing in order to kill them, and between the abode of the sea monsters **Scylla** and **Charybdis**, he sailed to the island Thrinacia ('three-pointed'), where his comrades, constrained by hunger, slew some cattle out of the sacred herds of **Hēlios**. In punishment for this the lightning of Zeus shattered the last ship, and only Odysseus, who had taken no part in the sacrilege, saved himself, reaching the island of Calypso after drifting about on the mast for nine days.

186. Alcinoüs, touched with sympathy at this narrative, now gives the much-tormented sufferer many gifts and sends him to Ithaca on a swift vessel. That he may not be recognized at once, his protectress Athena gives him the appearance of a beggar. In this form he hunts up his shepherd Eumaeus, and from him learns of the arrogance of his wife's suitors. Odysseus tells nobody except his son Telemachus who he is; but his old dog and his nurse Euryclea recognize him in spite of his metamorphosis, while he is staying in his own house as a beggar. Penelope has just announced that she will marry the one who can stretch the bow of her deceased husband and shoot an arrow through the openings of twelve axes placed in a row one behind another. All the suitors attempt in vain to bend the bow; but Odysseus easily accomplishes the feat. Being changed back to his proper form, he makes himself known, and with the assistance of his son and two faithful shepherds, Eumaeus and Philoetius, in a savage conflict, he puts all the suitors to the sword. Then for the first time Penelope learns of her husband's return. Finally Odysseus seeks out his old father Laërtes, who is cultivating a farm in the vicinity.

Chryseïs: Homer, Il. i. *passim;* Ovid, Ars Amat. ii. 402; Hyginus, Fab. cxxi.

Achilles: Homer, Il. i., *et passim;* Ovid, Amor. i. 9, 33, Rem. Amor. 777, Trist. iii. 5, 37; Hyginus, Fab. xcvi.; Shak., Love's Labour's Lost v. 2, 635, Troilus and Cressida *passim.*

Briseïs: Homer, Il. i., *et passim;* Ovid, Rem. Amor. 777, 783, Her. iii.; Hyginus, Fab. cvi.

Pandarus: Homer, Il. ii., *et passim;* Vergil, Aen. v. 496; Shak., Troilus and Cressida *passim.*

Diomedes: Homer, Il. ii., *et passim;* Ovid, Met. xiii. 100 *sq.;* Shak., Troilus and Cressida *passim.*

Ajax (son of Telamon): Homer, Il. ii., *et passim;* Sophocles, Ajax; Horace, Od. ii. 4, 5; Ovid, Met. xiii. 2:—

Clipei dominus septemplicis Aiax.

Hyginus, Fab. cvii., cxiv.; Shak., King Henry VI. pt. ii. v. 1, 26, Troilus and Cressida *passim.*

Nestor: Homer, Il. i., *et passim,* Od. iii. *passim;* Ovid, Met. xiii. 63; Shak., Rape of Lucrece 203:—

Nestor's golden words;

King Henry VI. pt. iii. iii. 2, 188, Troilus and Cressida *passim.*

Hector: Homer, Il. i., *et passim;* Ovid, Met. xii., xiii. *passim;* Euripides, Andromache; Vergil, Aen. i., ii. *passim;* Shak., Love's Labour's Lost v. 2, 537, King Henry IV. pt. ii. ii. 4, 237, King Henry VI. pt. iii. iv. 8, 25, Troilus and Cressida *passim.*

Priam: Homer, Il. xxii. *passim;* Ovid, Met. xiii. 470 *sq.;* Vergil, Aen. i., ii. *passim;* Hyginus, Fab. xc.; Shak., Hamlet ii. 2, 469, King Henry VI. pt. iii. ii. 5, 120, Troilus and Cressida *passim.*

Patroclus: Homer, Il. xvi., *et passim.*

Telemachus: Homer, Od. *passim;* Ovid, Her. i. 98, 107.

Calypso: Homer, Od. vii. 245: —

ἔνθα μὲν Ἄτλαντος θυγάτηρ, δολόεσσα Καλυψώ,

Od. i. 14, v. 77 *sq.;* Ovid, Amor. ii. 17, 15: —

Traditur et nymphe mortalis amore Calypso
Capta recusantem detinuisse virum.

Pope, Moral Essays ii. 45: —

'Twas thus Calypso once each heart alarm'd.

Odysseus (Ulysses): Homer, Il. ii. *passim*, Od. *passim;* Ovid, Ars Amat. ii. 123, Met. xiii. 124 *sq.;* Vergil, Aen. ii. *passim;* Hyginus, Fab. xcv., cxxv., cxxvi.; Shak., Rape of Lucrece 200: —

Sly Ulysses;

King Henry VI. pt. iii. iii. 2, 180, Coriolanus i. 3, 93, Troilus and Cressida *passim;* Pope, Argus 9: —

Forgot of all his own domestic crew:
The faithful dog alone his rightful master knew.

Penelope: Homer, Od. *passim;* Ovid, Her. i., Ars Amat. iii. 15; Hyginus, Fab. cxxvi.; Marlowe, Dr. Faustus v. 153: —

Chaste as was Penelope.

Shak., Coriolanus i. 3, 92.

Alcinoüs: Homer, Od. vi. 12, vii. *passim;* Ovid, Amor. i. 10, 55; Vergil, Geor. ii. 87; Horace, Epis. i. 2, 28.

Polyphemus: Homer, Od. i. 69 *sq.*, ix.; Ovid, Met. xiii. 765 *sq.*, xiv. 167, Ex Pont. ii. 2, 115; Vergil, Aen. iii. 641 *sq.;* Hyginus, Fab. cxxv.

Laestrygones: Ovid, Met. xiv. 233; Hyginus, Fab. cxxv.

Circe: Homer, Od. x. 136 *sq.;* Ovid, Met. xiv. 10 *sq.;* Vergil, Aen. vii. 20, 282; Keats, Endymion iii. 624: —

> Cursed, cursed Circe!
> O vulture-witch, hast never heard of mercy!

Chaucer, Knight's Tale 1086.

Sirenes: Homer, Od. xii. 167; Ovid, Met. v. 555 *sq.*, Ars Amat. iii. 311; Hyginus, Fab. cxli.; Milton, Comus 878:—

> And the songs of Sirens sweet.

Shak., Sonnet cxix.

Laërtes: Homer, Od. i. 430, *et passim;* Ovid, Her. i. 105, Met. xiii. 144.

D. THE ROMAN GODS

187. In religion, as in all other spheres of the spiritual life, the influence of Greece gradually displaced that which was really native in Rome, or at least filled the old, simple forms with new meaning. This process began as early as the reign of the two Tarquinii, when Greek ideas found entrance into Rome, partly through the Etruscans, and partly through the colonies of southern Italy, such as Cumae. From about the time of the second Punic war these ideas began to destroy entirely the old beliefs, at least in the better educated circles of society. At last, almost all the varieties of worship that existed anywhere within the borders of the mighty Roman Empire found their way to Rome. All the testimony that we possess in literature concerning the relations of the ancient Roman religion has been influenced by this Hellenizing tendency; and only the festival calendar, which had been made up before that period, and the existence of certain priesthoods whose institution dates back to the very earliest times furnish, concerning what is genuinely Roman, information that is trustworthy, though meagre. In the following statements these oldest testimonies will serve as landmarks, in order that, so far as possible, everything which forced its way from Greece into the Roman religion may be excluded.

I. DIVINITIES NOT REDUCED TO A UNIFORM CONCEPTION

188. In studying the beliefs of the Romans we find side by side with the regular deities a series of divinities who, without being reduced to a uniform conception or perfected to the point of enjoying a complete personality, continued to occupy the position of deified ancestors and of spirits (*daimones*).

(1) First among these should be mentioned the divinities representing souls : the **Mānēs**, **Lemurēs**, and **Lārvae**. Closely akin to these were the **Geniī**, who represented the vital force and power of procreation in men, and the **Jūnōnēs** of women, spirits corresponding in their nature to the Genii. They were supposed to enter the body at birth, and leave it at death; then they became Manes. Like the souls of the dead, the Genii were supposed to have the form of serpents. But the Genius and the Juno were also worshiped as the tutelary spirits of men and women, by whom oaths were ratified, and to whom sacrifices were offered on birthdays.

Starting from this idea of a tutelary spirit, conceived of as a person endowed with procreative power, the Romans afterwards came to attribute Genii to the family also, to the city, to the State, and at pleasure to every locality where a creative activity might manifest itself, and by this process made them practically representatives of the real divinities of nature.

189. An intermediate position like that of these Genii was occupied by a class of divinities essentially similar to them, the **Larēs**, who were regarded as tutelary spirits of fields, vineyards, roads, and groves, and at the same time were worshiped by usages that were in many respects quite characteristic of the worship of the dead. In earlier times we hear usually of only a single *Lār familiāris*, who protects and represents hearth and home; afterwards, however, they always appear in pairs. Little wooden images of them, very much alike, were placed above, or near, the hearth in the *ātrium;* and at every meal, and especially on the Calends, Nones, Ides, and at all family festivals, the matron of the house offered to them a little food and a fresh wreath.

Under the term *deī Penātēs*, divinities whose images were likewise placed near the hearth, were included all the gods that were regarded as protectors of the provisions (*penus*) in the house, without its being necessarily true that the same gods were everywhere meant. Janus, Juppiter, and Vesta, are named among them. From the individual house their functions, like those of the Genii, were transferred to society in common, and consequently *Penātēs pūblicī* were worshiped on the common hearth in the temple of Vesta.

190. (2) Divinities entirely peculiar to the Roman faith, not represented as having any distinguishing characteristics as individuals, were the **Indigetēs** ('those acting within'), *i.e.* whatsoever spirits were supposed to bring about individual acts in particular persons or things. To each one of these divinities only a single, strictly defined action was ascribed, which was exactly expressed by the divinity's name; it was therefore necessary to take heed to call for help upon exactly the right Indiges, and at the right moment. Consequently the Pontifices, a college of priests who had a decisive superintendence over these matters, as well as over other questions of worship, in their effort to attain exactness and definiteness, developed an almost endless series of such spirits of activity after the pattern of a few ancient forms of this sort, particularly, it seems, during the fourth century b.c. Because of this very exaggeration in their number and importance they soon lost their significance; at any rate, the worship of the Indigetes had by the time of the second Punic war fallen into disuse. How subtle these distinctions were may be seen, for example, in the fact that on the occasion of a child's first leaving the house it was considered necessary to invoke Abeona, on its return, Adeona, and at the same time also Domiduca and Iterduca.

II. DEIFIED FORCES OF NATURE, AND DIVINITIES CLOSELY RELATED TO SPIRITS OF ACTIVITY

191. (1) Among the Romans the only proper divinities of nature with fully individualized personality were the representatives of the forces operating in **springs** and **rivers**. As in Greece, the divinities of springs were usually thought of as female beings; they were worshiped in the groves surrounding the springs, but even in very early times were also developed into goddesses of prophecy and song, and into such as come to help difficult births. From the idea of their relation to prophecy and song the Camenae, who dwelt in a grove outside the *Porta Capēna*, came to be identified with the Greek Muses; while the prophesying spouse of king Numa, Egeria, who was closely connected with the Camenae, and dwelt in the same grove, was principally invoked in the capacity of a goddess of birth. The essential characteristics of both these types were combined in Carmenta, the mother of Evander, who probably derived her name from *Carmen* ('prophecy'). But the spring goddess Juturna, whose name was borne by several springs in Latium, came to be regarded as the wife of Janus and the mother of Fons or Fontus, *i.e.* of the spring itself conceived of as a god.

192. Among **river gods** at Rome *pater Tiberīnus* enjoyed the highest honors. A special priestly college, the *Pontificēs* ('bridge-makers'), was commissioned with the duty of keeping in repair the *pōns sublicius, i.e.* the bridge on piles leading over the river. The authority of the Pontifices was so great that they gradually rose into the position of a general court of control over all religious affairs. The very early period of their origin is indicated by a decision that no iron should be employed in putting up the bridge. The annual sacrifice of the so-called Argeï was also of very ancient origin. On this occasion in later times figures made of rushes were cast from the bridge into the stream as a substitute for the earlier custom of sacrificing human beings. In Lavinium the god of the Numicius was worshiped; in Umbria, the Clitumnus; in Campania, the Volturnus.

193. Compared with these divinities, who were associated with individual springs or individual rivers, **Neptūnus** ('Neptune'), the representative of water in general, stood apparently, in the earlier period, quite in the background. Nevertheless, in the hottest month, on the 23d of July, the *Neptūnālia* were celebrated in his honor, probably to induce him to dispense the much-needed moisture. He first came to be considered the god of the sea by being identified with Poseidon, whose worship was introduced into Rome in the year 399 B.C. by order of the Sibylline books.

194. (2) Among the gods that were worshiped from the earliest times the following are pretty closely related to the spirits of activity discussed above: Janus, the spirit of the door arch (*jānus*), or of the house door as a whole (*jānua*); Vesta, the goddess of the hearth fire; Volcanus, the exciter of conflagrations; the war god Mars; the gods of sowing and reaping, Saturnus and Consus; and the series of gods and goddesses whose activity is manifested in the growth of plants.

Jānus, from being the tutelary spirit of the individual door, developed into the representative of entering, in general, and so became the god of beginning (indeed, both these ideas were expressed by the Romans in the single word *initium*). Therefore the beginning of the day and of the month, *i.e.* morning (*Jānus Mātūtīnus*) and the *Kalendae*, were sacred to him. His month, *Jānuārius*, which is coincident with the beginning of increase in the length of days, was at a comparatively late period promoted to the position of being the beginning of the year proper.[1] On the 9th of January, the date of the sacrificial festival (*Agōnium*) celebrated in his honor, the bellwether of a flock was sacrificed to him, originally by the king himself,—who evidently, on the transfer of the domestic worship of Janus to the State, became the representative of the father of the family,—afterwards by the *rēx sacrōrum*. Janus was invoked at the commencement of all actions, particularly at the beginning of

---

[1] Diva Angerona, whose worship was celebrated on the 21st of December, and who was represented with mouth bound or covered with a finger (*favēte linguis!*), was perhaps an ancient goddess of the fortunate commencement of the year. But Anna Peranna (or Perenna), the goddess of continuing years, whose festival was kept on the 15th of March, is to be regarded as the representative of the new year.

prayers and offerings; indeed, he was regarded even at a very early period as the *principium*, and the father of the gods.

195. The chief sanctuary of this god, the *Jānus Geminus*, or *Quirīnus*, situated at the north end of the Forum, opposite the sanctuary of Vesta, which served as the common hearth of the State, was the very ancient arched doorway or entrance of the Forum, which was itself patterned after the *ātrium* of a house. The doors on the two sides of the passageway were kept open as long as an army was in the field, probably for the reason that at one time the king himself used to march with his troops to war, and it was necessary that the city gate should stand open for him until his return, as the house door did for the father of the family. Under the archway stood an image of the god with two faces, one looking outward and one inward. Although this image was probably patterned after Greek models, yet it is clear that the intention was to express by it the attentiveness and watchfulness which are characteristic of a doorkeeper. Like a real *jānitor* ('doorkeeper'), he carried a key and a switch or staff (*virga*) for driving away troublesome intruders; and the nature of his activity was indicated by the epithets *Patulcius* ('opener'), and *Clūsivius* or *Clūsius* ('closer').

His other principal ancient place of worship was the hill named for him Janiculum, on which king Ancus Marcius had built a fortress, to protect the commercial road leading into Etruria, and the harbor in the Tiber situated at its foot. So from being the god of entrance and departure he became the protector of commerce and navigation; his head and the prow of a ship were stamped on the oldest Roman coin, the *ās;* and afterwards representations of the special god of harbors, Portunus, were made to imitate this well-known Janus type.

196. Like the Hestia of the Greeks, **Vesta** embodied the power manifesting itself in the hearth fire; and the hearth fire itself was worshiped as a goddess, without any special image. The city also had its common hearth, with its Vesta and its Penates. At Rome this was situated in a small circular temple on the south side of the Forum. The service of the goddess was attended to by six maidens, who, being chosen in childhood by the Pontifex Maximus, were required to remain unmarried for thirty years. If one of these Vestal virgins allowed the sacred fire to go out, or became guilty of unchastity, the severest penalties were inflicted upon her by the Pontifex Maximus. The sacred fire could be newly kindled only by means of the old fire drill, or, afterwards, by the burning glass. The *Vestālia,* the principal festival of the goddess, came on the 9th of June, and on this day the matrons offered sacrifices of food on the common hearth.

197. In contrast to Vesta, who occupied the position of a benefactress, yet supplementary to her, was **Volcānus,** the representative of the power of fire that destroys all the works of men's hands, *i.e.* the god of conflagrations. Since it was necessary that he should be kept removed from the houses of the city, he had his temple outside the walls, in the Campus Martius. His principal festival was celebrated on the 23d of August, at the time when, after the ingathering of the harvest, the full granaries especially needed his protection. In order that he might subdue a fire that had once broken out, he was called in flattery *Mulciber, mītis* or *quiētus*. He may have been connected with the fire of the lightning at first because this causes conflagrations; but, since in ancient prayers he was invoked in conjunction with Maia, the goddess of the fruitfulness of the ground, whose worship was celebrated in May, it seems probable that other results of his activity in the fire of the lightning and of the sun were recognized. It was not until later times that he became the god of the smith's art and of volcanoes, and then only by being identified with Hephaestus.

198. Like Volcanus, the divinities that protected agriculture, Saturnus, Consus, and Ops, retained their character as spirits of activity. **Sāturnus**, or Saëturnus, was the god of sowing; after the sowing of the winter grain was finished, the feast of the *Sāturnālia* was celebrated in his honor from the 17th to the 21st or 23d of December, with banqueting, the interchange of presents, and exemption of the slaves from their customary duties. The wax candles that were regularly included among the gifts undoubtedly symbolized the newly-beginning increase of sunlight, which gave ground for the hope that the seed buried in the ground would thrive. The ancient sanctuary of Saturn, and his temple, which was built by Tarquinius Superbus, were situated beside the ascent that led from the Forum to the Capitol. **Cōnsus**, on the other hand, was the harvest god, the *deus condendī, i.e.* god of stowing away the produce of the fields. As this produce was originally kept in subterranean rooms, the old altar of Consus in the Circus Maximus was usually concealed in the ground, and was uncovered and cleared for use in sacrifice only during the festivals of the *Cōnsuālia*, which were celebrated with running matches on the 21st of August and the 15th of December.

With Consus is intimately associated *Ops Cōnsīva, i.e.* **Ops,** the wife of Consus. She represented the *opīma frūgum cōpia,* the abundance of the products that were stored away at harvest time; her two feasts, the *Opicōnsīvia* and the *Opālia,* were separated from those of her husband by intervals of only three days in each case. At a later period Saturn was identified with Cronus, and Ops with Rhea, and many peculiarities of the Greek forms of their worship were transferred to this worship in Rome.

199. (3) The vital forces operating in forest and field were ascribed to the activity of various impregnating gods and conceiving goddesses. The country people and shepherds believed that they owed to these divinities the products of the ground and the abundance of their flocks, and worshiped them; and the divinities, as did their worshipers, had their favorite abodes in shady groves and at bubbling springs. Their nature was as simple and rustic as the mind of the worshipers, and everything dear and precious to the countryman was committed to their protecting care.

Faunus was the husband or father of Fauna, who was usually invoked as *Bona Dea.* His name signifies 'the benevolent god,' being derived from *favēre* ('to be gracious'). He appeared in human form under the name Evander (Gk. *Euandros,* 'good man'), who was said to have established the first settlement on the site where Rome was afterwards located. It was also told of this Evander that he had founded the oldest sanctuary of Faunus in a grotto on the Palatine hill, and instituted the feast of the *Luper-*

cālia, which was celebrated there on the 15th of February, at which the Luperci, *i.e.* the priests of *Faunus Lupercus* ('little wolf'), girded with goatskins, but otherwise naked, tried to secure fruitfulness for man, beast, and field by running round the ancient limits of the town's territory. In harmony with this custom Faunus himself was represented naked, with goatskin, garland, cornucopia, and drinking horn.

200. Very closely related to Faunus was **Silvānus**, the spirit of the forest; but his activity, as his name indicates, was confined exclusively to the forest, and therefore in his representations in art he wears a pine wreath, and carries a pine branch on his arm. He, as well as Faunus, frightened the lonesome wanderer by the prophesying voices of the forest. Silvanus especially protected boundaries and property in general.

In the luxuriant productiveness of the fields and vineyards the Romans thought they saw the particular activity of **Līber** and his wife **Lībera**, who, like Juppiter *Līber*, being designated by their names bountiful dispensers of plenty, were afterwards regularly identified with Dionysus and Persephone. The name of the latter was changed in Italy to the form Proserpina.

Similarly, gardens and their fruit trees were under the special protection of **Vertumnus**, who was supposed to change his form as the gardens themselves changed their appearance in the varying seasons, and of **Pōmōna**, the beautiful dispenser of fruits, either of whom could be recognized by the ever present pruning knife.

201. Among the goddesses of fruitfulness **Fauna** (**Bona Dea**) took precedence. Her most noted sanctuary at Rome was situated at the foot of the Aventine hill. The anniversary of its establishment was celebrated on the first of May. Her chief festival, however, was kept with secret sacrifices by the vestal virgins and the noble women of Rome, all men being excluded, at the beginning of December, in the house of a praetor or a consul, who in this function probably had taken the place earlier allotted to the king. In works of art she appears as a woman in a sitting posture, fully clothed; like her husband Faunus, she carries in her arms a cornucopia.

Besides Libera and Pomona, who have already been mentioned, Feronia, Flora, Pales, and perhaps Diana, were closely related to the Bona Dea.

Fērōnia was a goddess of central Italy, whose worship was carried on chiefly in a grove near Capena, not far from Mount Soracte in Etruria, and in a similar one near Tarracina, in the vicinity of the Pontine marshes. At Rome a festival in her honor was kept about the middle of November in the Campus Martius. She was always invoked as a giver of the blessings of the harvest; and, inasmuch as at all harvest festivals the slaves enjoyed many liberties, the emancipation of slaves was frequently accomplished in the temple of this goddess.

202. Flōra, who likewise was indigenous to central Italy, was in the narrower sense a goddess of flowers, and then, by a natural development of the thought, a dispenser of fruitfulness. At Rome she had a very ancient temple on the Quirinal hill. On the 28th of April the flower festival (*Flōrālia*) was celebrated with wanton dances and coarse jests; after a while scenic games and games of the circus were added to the festivities. With her was associated Robigus, the god that protected the grain from the *rōbīgō* ('rust').

Palēs was the special tutelary goddess of pastures and herds of cattle, as her name indicates, being connected with *pā-scō* ('to pasture') (*cf.* Pan). In Rome the seat of her worship was on the *Palātium* (Palatine hill), which was probably named after her. On the 21st of April the *Palīlia* (or *Parīlia*) were celebrated in her honor, a feast at which sheep and stables were purified and consecrated by water and bloodless sacrifices. For the same purpose shepherds and flocks leaped over heaps of burning straw. A similar custom prevailed at the feast of Feronia, and is still in vogue in Germany at the bonfires on Easter eve and St. John's day.

203. Diāna should probably be added to this series of goddesses of fruitfulness. Like all the others, she was worshiped in well-watered groves (Diana *Nemorēnsis*), especially on Mount Tifata, near Capua, and in the vicinity of Tusculum, near Aricia. At Aricia the custom was for him to succeed to the priesthood who should slay his predecessor with a bough broken in the sacred grove. This was evidently a kind of human sacrifice which was offered with the assistance of the goddess herself, who manifested her power in her trees. At Rome her ancient temple was situated on the Aventine. Here, and throughout Italy, her principal feast was kept on the Ides of August, a day on which sacrifices were offered to Vertumnus also. In Aricia there was a torchlight procession in the early morning to honor her, just as Pales was worshiped at sunrise, and Flora by lighting candles.[1] Like Feronia, she protected slaves, evidently those especially that had fled into the forest which was

---

[1] Mater Matuta, for whom the *Mātrālia* ('mother festival') were observed, was, like Diana, a goddess both of the dawn and of birth.

consecrated to her, and were pursued like fleeing stags. Like the Bona Dea, moreover, she was especially worshiped by women and was besought as the giver of fecundity and an easy birth. This phase of her character, perhaps, accounts for the fact that several of her temples, for example, those at Tusculum, Aricia, and Rome, were sanctuaries of confederacies of various Latin tribes. At a later period Diana, as goddess of groves and fruitfulness, was fully identified with Artemis, and thus became a goddess of the hunt, and a moon goddess, an idea which, so far as the indigenous Diana is concerned, could have had no foundation except in her feast on the Ides.

204. (4) It is more doubtful what position was originally occupied by **Mārs**, who from the earliest times was worshiped in all the tribes of central Italy. Various things go to show that he was an old sun god, *viz.* his close relationship to the Greek Apollo; certain ancient formulas of supplication, in which he is entreated to protect and bless the fields, crops, vineyards, etc.; and the dedication of the so-called *vēr sacrum, i.e.* the offering of the next spring's expected increase in human beings, cattle, and crops, which was promised at times of severe disaster. On the other hand, he was closely enough related to the spirits of activity to represent principally, at least in later times, the divine power exerted in war. But his efficacy in war was not restricted to so narrow a province as was that of the Indigetes of later times, who were creations of the elaborate wisdom of the priests. His name Mars, or Mavors, and his ancient epithet *Gradīvus* cannot be explained with certainty; but it is evident from his old symbolic attributes, and from what we know of his feasts, that he was regarded as a god of war even in very early times.

205. In the royal residence of the old Romans, the Regia, were kept the sacred spears of Mars and a shield (*ancīle*) which fell from heaven. King Numa had eleven other shields made like this. The twelve Palatine Salii ('leapers'), or priests of Mars, each provided with one of these shields, in the month sacred to the god (March) performed armed dances, chanting an ancient song. The significance of his other feasts indicates that this celebration probably marked the beginning of the season for war, which was restricted to the summer. On the 27th of February and the 14th of March, near the old altar of Mars, situated in the midst of the Campus Martius, the *Equīria* were held, which consisted in a review of horses, and a chariot race. On the 19th and the 23d of March, at the feast of *Quīnquātrūs* and of *Tubilūstrium*, the weapons and war trumpets were inspected and purified. Likewise on the 19th of October, after the close of the war season, a purification of weapons (*Armilūstrium*) took place, while the sacrifice of the October horse evidently corresponded to the *Equīria* of the spring; for the horse that had been victorious at the preceding chariot race was on the 15th of October sacrificed to Mars.

The wolf, the emblem of murder attended by bloodshed, was considered sacred to Mars; likewise the woodpecker (*pīcus*), which produced the impression of being a warlike creature by his bill (which pierces into the trees as a battering-ram bores through the gates), and by the feathery, plumelike adornment of his head. Here we find the explanation of the legend that a she-wolf nourished Romulus and Remus; for the war god himself was their father, and, accordingly, the ancestor of the warlike Romans.

206. Quirinus, the chief god of the Sabines, who settled on the Quirinal hill, was so closely related to the old Latin Mars that the worship of the two gods easily blended. Yet side by side with the *flāmen Mārtiālis* (Mars's especial priest) there continued to exist a separate *flāmen Quirīnālis;* and besides the Palatine Salii of Mars there were twelve Salii peculiar to Quirinus, who had their abode on the Quirinal. While Mars was regarded as the father of Romulus, Quirinus was afterwards identified with Romulus himself. That he was also considered a tribal god seems to be indicated further by the festival customs of the *Quirīnālia*, which were celebrated on the 17th of February.

Janus: Ovid, Fast. i. 64 *sq.*, ii. 49 *sq.*, vi. 119; Vergil, Aen. vii. 180, 610, viii. 357; Horace, Epis. ii. 1, 255; Milton, Par. L. xi. 127: —

> With him the cohort bright
> Of watchful cherubim; four faces each
> Had, like a double Janus.

Vesta; Vestal Virgins: Fire worship was a special feature of Indo-European religious conception. We find this tendency more or less marked in all the representatives of the race. From the smothered spark to the orb of day, adoration was given to this all-purifying, changing element. The Hindu looked upon the fire as an intercessory priest that would carry his oblation to heaven. In the Persian religion fire was the mysterious symbol demanding veneration. This idea is emphasized in the Avesta. In the tomb of Darius at Naqshi Rustam, opposite the figure of the king is the altar with the sacred fire blazing. This same conception of the sanctity of fire gave rise to the story of Prometheus among the Greeks, and established the holy fire at the Roman temple of Vesta. The first hymn of the Rig Veda describes the priesthood of fire, from which the few following stanzas are translated. Rig Veda i. 1: —

1. Agni I praise the household priest the heavenly lord of sacrifice, |
The Hotar most generous in blessings.
2. Agni as by ancient seers so by recent ones is to be praised, |
He shall bring hither the gods.
4. What holy sacrifice thou, O Agni, art encompassing, |
That goes among the gods.
9. As a father to a son, so, O Agni, be accessible to us, |
Accompany us into well-being.

Ovid, Met. xv. 864, Fast. iii. 45, vi. 713 *sq.*; Vergil, Geor. i. 498, iv. 384, Aen. ii. 296, 567; Macaulay, Battle of Lake Regillus 35.

Bona Dea: Ovid, Ars Amat. iii. 244.

Silvanus: Ovid, Met. xiv. 639; Vergil, Ecl. x. 24; Spenser, F. Q. i. vi. 14.

Vertumnus: Ovid, Met. xiv. 642 *sq.*; Pope, Vertumnus and Pomona; Keats, Endymion ii. 444: —

> Taste these juicy pears
> Sent me by sad Vertumnus, when his fears
> Were high about Pomona.

Pomona: Ovid, Met. xiv. 623 *sq.*; Pope, Windsor Forest, 37: —
> See Pan with flocks, with fruits Pomona crowned;

Vertumnus and Pomona; Macaulay, Prophecy of Capys 18.

Flora: Ovid, Fast. v. 195: —
> Chloris eram, quae Flora vocor.

Spenser, F. Q. i. iv. 17.

Pales: Ovid, Fast. iv. 722 *sq.*; Macaulay, Prophecy of Capys 18.

Mars Gradivus: Ovid, Ars Amat. ii. 566, Fast. ii. 861, iii. 169; Vergil, Aen. x. 542.

III. DIVINITIES OF THE HEAVENS

207. Mightier than all the divinities of the earth, who have just been discussed, appear to have been the representatives of those forces that operate in the heavens and in the air. In Italy these forces were embodied in the divine pair, Juppiter and Juno. The former was, perhaps, considered the god whose power was exercised in the sky, preferably by day; the latter, a moon goddess, who ruled by night.

The mightiest phenomenon that takes place in the atmosphere is the thunderstorm; therefore **Juppiter**, to whose agency this was traced, like Zeus among the Greeks, was considered the most powerful god, who held everything else under his sway. He carried the lightning as his weapon, and in the earliest times in particular forms of worship was even called by the name *Fulgur* ('lightning'). He was the giver of signs by means of lightning and by birds, the observation and the interpretation of which was the duty of the college of priests called Augurs. He also sent the fructifying thundershowers, and in times of prolonged drouth was invoked under the name *Ēlicius* ('the one that entices forth' the rain). At the same time he came to be considered as the giver of fruitfulness and of luxuriant plenteousness, whose chief characteristic was *Līberālitās* ('generosity'). When so regarded he enjoyed the epithet *Līber*. The celebration of the festivals relating to the culture of the vine was in his honor, *viz*. the *Vīnālia Rūstica* on the 19th of August, the *Meditrīnālia* on the 11th of October, and the *Vīnālia* on the 23d of April; agriculture, cattle-raising, and young people just getting their growth were under his protection; and a chapel of Juventas ('youth') was accordingly located in his temple on the Capitoline hill.

208. On the other hand the phenomena of the thunderstorm that threaten men with danger and destruction were ascribed to a divinity that was distinguished from Juppiter, *viz*. **Vējovis** or **Vēdjovis**, *i.e.* the evil Juppiter. His sanctuary was situated between the two summits of the Capitoline. He was represented as a youth with a bunch of thunderbolts or arrows in his hand.

Summānus also, the god of the thunderstorms which come up in the night *sub māne* ('towards morning'), was but a secondary form of Juppiter. It is still doubtful whether the old epithet *Lūcetius* ('light-bringer') did, as is usually assumed, characterize Juppiter as the god of the light of the sky, or whether this name, too, should be referred to the light of the thunderbolt, the lightning.

209. The mighty god of the thunderstorm, under the name of Juppiter *Stator*, became a helper in battle, and under the epithet *Victor* was considered the bestower of victory. Victorious generals offered to Juppiter *Feretrius* as a gift the *spolia opīma*, *i.e.* the armor of the opposing commander whom they had slain with their own hands. His servants were the Fetiales, who with solemn ceremonies demanded satisfaction for injuries, declared wars, and concluded treaties; for his lightning-flash punished the perjured one who violated a treaty. For this reason Juppiter was invoked as the god of oaths of other kinds; Dius Fidius, the god of fidelity, was regarded as the Genius of Juppiter, and the sanctuary of Fides (*i.e.* 'fidelity' conceived of as a goddess) from the earliest times stood close beside his temple on the Capitoline. In this temple, moreover, was the sacred boundary stone, the emblem of Terminus, in order that Juppiter might be recognized as the protector of boundaries and property.

One of the oldest sanctuaries where the worship of Juppiter was carried on was a sacred grove on the summit of the *Mōns Albānus*, where formerly the Latin communities had united themselves under the leadership of Alba Longa for the worship of Juppiter *Latiāris*, the protector of Latium. The younger Tarquinius, who built the temple on the Capitoline, likewise erected one on this very spot. Here the *Fēriae Latīnae* were celebrated with sacrifices and games; and commanders to whom the senate had refused a regular triumph at the Capitol often marched to this sanctuary to offer their spoils of war.

210. But after Rome had gained the leadership over Latium, the temple on the southern summit of the Capitoline became the most important place of Juppiter's worship; for, as Rome itself dictated its commands to the world, so the Roman Juppiter *Capitōlīnus*, or J. *Optimus Māximus*, ruled over heaven and earth. He was the proper lord and protector of the free city; therefore the victorious home-returning commander rendered to him fitting thanks, and, arrayed with the attributes and raiment of the god, marched in triumph up to the Capitol, to lay the victor's laurel in the lap of the god who gave the victory, and to dedicate the most valuable part of the booty to his temple. The most important games, the *Lūdī Māgnī*, out of which the *Lūdī Rōmānī* and the *Lūdī Plēbēī* were afterwards developed, were celebrated in his honor.

211. Side by side with the worship of Juppiter upon the Capitoline was that of his wife Juno and his daughter Minerva. His temple, accordingly, had a threefold cella, the central division belonging to Juppiter himself, the one on his left to Juno, and that on his right to Minerva. The association of the three divinities was, to be sure, entirely Greek in its origin, but was adopted in Etruria, and thence carried over to Rome towards the close of the epoch of the kings.

The first minister of Juppiter was the *flāmen Diālis*, who offered sacrifices on all the Ides (days of full moon), all of which were sacred to Juppiter, and at all the other feasts of this god; the *flāminica*, wife of the *flāmen*, was the priestess of Juno. Their married life was supposed to emblematize that of the divine pair whom they represented.

212. The worship of **Jūnō**, which was common throughout Italy from ancient times, was very prominent among the Latins, Oscans, and Umbrians. With the Latins, one month, *Jūnius* or *Jūnōnius*, was named after her, and on its Calends the feast of Juno *Monēta* ('the reminding') was kept at Rome, probably to celebrate her marriage with Juppiter.

Juno Moneta had an ancient temple on the Capitoline, and in the inclosure belonging to this were kept the sacred geese known as the rescuers of the city. As the wife of Juppiter *Rēx* she was called *Rēgīna*; her son Mars was born on the first of March, the date on which the women celebrated in her honor the *Mātrōnālia* ('mother festival'). Moreover, all the Calends (days of new moon) were sacred to her, probably because she was originally a moon goddess. To this fact her epithets *Lūcetia* and *Lūcīna* ('light-bringer') refer, though under the latter name she was usually invoked as the goddess of childbirth. Juno *Lūcīna*, who in works of art often carries in her arms a child in swaddling clothes, had a very ancient grove on the Esquiline, and was worshiped extensively all over Italy. As goddess of marriage she was called also Juno *Juga* or *Jugālis* ('the conjugal'), or *Prōnuba* ('bridesmaid'). Her epithet *Sōspita*, which was current especially at Lanuvium, designated her a protectress or savior in general. When so represented, she is armed with shield and spear, and wears a goatskin over her head, shoulders, and back. Juno *Rēgīna*, like Juppiter *Rēx*, carries the scepter as a distinctive attribute.

Lucina: Ovid, Fast. ii. 449: —

> Gratia Lucinae. dedit haec tibi nomina lucus,
> Aut quia principium tu, Dea, lucis habes.

Horace, Car. Saec. 15: —

> Sive tu Lucina, probas vocari
> Seu Genitalis.

Shak., Pericles iii. 1, 10, Cymbeline v. 4, 43; Chaucer, Knight's Tale 1227.

IV. DIVINITIES OF DEATH

213. The idea of a general realm of the dead did not become thoroughly prevalent at Rome, as has been shown in § 9; and accordingly no divinities conceived of as rulers of such a domain were independently developed among the Romans. The coming of death itself, however, was ascribed to the activity of a god who ruled sometimes terribly, and again gently, who was named **Orcus**, although his form was not fully perfected in the minds of his worshipers. Besides him there appeared under various appellations a motherly guardian of the dead, who was probably really Mother [1] Earth (*Tellūs* or *Terra Māter*), inasmuch as she received the dead into her bosom. From the Manes and Lares she was named Mania, Lara or Larunda; from the Larvae, *Avia Lārvārum* ('grandmother of ghosts'), and like them was represented as of frightful form. Finally, on account of the silence of

---

[1] Tellus was worshiped as a mother especially by means of the *Fordicīdia*, a sacrifice of pregnant cows.

the dead, she was called *Dea Mūta* or *Tacita* ('the dumb or silent goddess'). Perhaps it would be best to place in this group Acca Larentia (mother of the Lares?) also, to whom funeral sacrifices were offered at the feast of the *Lārentālia* (23d of December); for her attributes seem to characterize her, like Tellus, as a goddess of the fruitfulness of the ground. (For **Libitīna** see § 216.)

Tellus: Ovid, Met. i. 80; Vergil, Aen. iv. 166; Shak., Hamlet iii. 2, 166, Pericles iv. 1, 14.

V. PERSONIFICATIONS

214. By transferring to the spiritual and moral realm the same kind of conceptions which had called forth belief in the spirits of activity (Indigetes), the Romans very early reached the point of worshiping actual personifications. To the oldest of these belong the following: Fortuna (the goddess of 'fortune'), usually distinguished by a rudder and a cornucopia; Fides ('fidelity'), with ears of corn and a fruit basket; Concordia ('harmony'), with a horn of plenty and a cup; Honos and Virtus (the god of 'honor' and the female representative of 'valor'), both in full armor; Spes ('hope'), with a flower in her hand; Pudicitia ('chastity'), veiled; and Salus ('deliverance,' 'safety'). Afterwards were added Pietas ('love of parents'), Libertas ('freedom'), Febris ('goddess of fevers'), Clementia ('mildness'), with cup and scepter, Pax ('goddess of peace'), with the olive branch. Finally, in the imperial epoch, it became the custom to personify any abstract idea whatever in the form of a woman distinguished by fitting attributes.

VI. DIVINITIES ORIGINALLY FOREIGN

215. Towards the end of the epoch of the kings the Etruscan culture, and with it, and through its agency, the culture of Greece, which already prevailed in southern Italy, began to exert an influence at Rome also. The Sibylline books, originating at Cumae, and containing a collection of Greek oracles, were particularly instrumental in introducing into Rome the worship of a whole multitude of Greek divinities. As the process went on, either the distinguishing characteristics of the foreign divinities were transferred to those of the native spirits of activity to which they were by nature closely related, or with the foreign ideas the foreign names also were borrowed. So **Minerva** originally, in all probability, represented only the divine power that produces thought and understanding in the human race, and was, at the same time, the protectress of expert workmanship. Her reception into the trinity (§ 211) worshiped at the Capitol she owed entirely to her identification with Pallas Athena, whose characteristics were now attributed to Minerva, except that she did not become properly a war goddess.

216. Venus, likewise, whose name is connected with *venustus* ('charming'), was not worshiped at Rome in the oldest times; it was the Greek Aphrodite, coming from southern Italy, and afterwards from Mount Eryx in Sicily, that found entrance into Rome under that name. Her oldest temple was in the grove of Libitina, a goddess of desire and of death; and her epithets, *Murcia* and *Cloācīna*, were undoubtedly borrowed from particular localities.

Mercurius may have been at first that particular one of the Indigetes who was considered the god of *merx* and *mercātūra, i.e.* the spirit of 'traffic.' By being identified with Hermes he became, for the first time, a fully developed god. But since he always remained far more exclusively the god of merchants than Hermes was, the money bag was his constant attribute in Italy.

The case was similar with Hercules: *Hēraklēs*, the favorite son of Zeus, and the dispenser of rural fruitfulness, was confused with the begetting Genius of Juppiter (who was supposed to have a Genius just as truly as every man had). Thus characterized he was united in wedlock with that Juno who represented the creative power of woman. But afterwards the purely Grecian form of the myth was so completely intermingled with this exclusively Italian conception that, in view of the enmity prevailing between Hera and Herakles, all sorts of contradictions resulted.

217. On the contrary, the worship of **Cerēs** at Rome was purely Greek. To be sure the name is closely connected with *crescere* and *creāre*, but the divine person was no more nor less than Demeter, who under that name was introduced into Rome in 496 B.C., and whose worship was so little altered in form that even in Rome her priestesses were required to be Greek women.

Still older, but likewise purely Greek, was the worship of **Apollō**, in whose honor the *lūdī Apollināres* were celebrated on the 13th of July after 212 B.C., in consequence of an oracle of the Sibylline books. *Dīs pater*, likewise, the ruler of the lower world, and the husband of Proserpina, was Pluto-Hades, appropriated bodily and unchanged by the Romans; *Dīs* is *dīves* ('the rich') a translation of *Plūtō*.

218. In the year 204 B.C. the sacred stone of the Magna Mater Idaea, *i.e.* of Ma or Ammas, was brought from Pessinus to Rome. In 186 B.C. the worship of Bacchus, which had degenerated on account of its excesses, was of necessity forcibly suppressed. Then Isis and Sarapis came in from Alexandria; and, finally, among many less important systems of worship, the *Mysteries* ('secret worship') of the Persian sun god Mithras were introduced, into which had already been incorporated many of the ideas and usages of Christianity, which was by this time victoriously advancing. Thus Christianity itself, as in Greece, so also in Rome, found a soil well prepared for its vigorous growth.

Sibylla: Ovid, Met. xiv. 104, 154; Vergil, Aen. vi. 98, 176; Pope, Dunciad iii. 15: —
    A slip-shod Sibyl led his steps along.
Shak., Taming of the Shrew i. 2, 70, Othello iii. 4, 70.

INDEX

[Of several references under one head, the most important one is placed first, in full-faced type. References to literary passages stand last, also in full-faced type. The numbers refer to sections, except when preceded by the letter p.]

Acamās 157
Acastus 162
Acca Lārentia 213
Achelōus **146**, 76, **p. 62**
Acherōn 6, 7, **p. 7**
Achillēs **177** sq., 2, 58, 131, **p. 141**
Achilleus v. Achillēs
Ācrisius 128
Actaeōn 57, **p. 50**
Admētus 162, **p. 128**
Adōnis 106, **p. 85**
Adrastus **171**, 74, 173
Aea 161, 163
Aeacus 8, **p. 9**
Aeētēs **164** sq., 161, **p. 128**
Aegeus **151** sq., 154, 165
aegis **23**, 35, 40
Aegisthus 130 *sq.*, **p. 103**
Aeglē 103, **p. 78**
Aegyptus 126 *sq.*
Aëllō 43
Aenēās 107, **p. 86**
Aeolus **44**, 184, **p. 38**
Aesculāpius **102**, 51, **p. 78**
Aesōn 161, **p. 128**
Aethra 151, **p. 122**
Agamemnōn **131**, 177 *sq.*, **p. 103**
Aganippē 114

Agēnōr **123**, 62, **p. 96**
Aglaïa 113
Aglauros **38**, 117
Agōnium 194
Aïdēs v. Hādēs
Aïdōneus v. Hādēs
Aisa 118
Ājāx 179, **p. 141**
Alcēstis 162, **p. 128**
Alceus 136
Alcīdēs 136
Alcinoüs **186**, 184, **p. 142**
Alcmaeōn **174**, 171
Alcmēnē **136**, 29
Alphēus 76, **p. 62**
Althaea 159, **p. 123**
Amalthēa **30**, 146
Amāzones **58**, 133, 141, 155, **p. 51**
Amazons v. Amāzones
ambrosia 28
Ammas v. Ma
Amor v. Erōs
Amphiarāus 171 *sq.*, **p. 133**
Amphictyonia 72
Amphīōn 124 *sq.*, **p. 96**
Amphitrītē **70**, 72, **p. 61**
Amphitryōn 136 *sq.*, **p. 116**
Amycus 166

Anchīsēs 107, **p. 86**
ancīlia 205
Androgeōs 153
Andromeda 128, **p. 102**
Angerōna 194
Anna Perenna 194
Antaeus 142, **p. 117**
Anthestēria **87**, 89, 95
Antigonē **173**, 170, **p. 133**
Antiopē **124**, 29, 62
Apatē 14
Aphrodītē **105 sq.**, 33, 81, 117, 160, 179, 216, **p. 85**
Aphroditos 107
Apollō **49 sq.**, 29, 54, 57, 125, 136, 144, 178, 180, 204, 217, **p. 49**
Apsyrtus 165, **p. 128**
Arachnē 39, **p. 33**
Arēs **116 sq.**, 24, 28, 105, 163, 164, **p. 89**
Arethūsa 76, **p. 62**
Argēī 192
Argēs 21
Argō 161, **p. 128**
Argonauts 161 *sq.*, **p. 128**
Argus 126, **p. 102**
Ariadnē **153**, 92, 158, **p. 74**
Arīōn **74**, 173
Aristaeus **50**, 57, **p. 50**
Armilūstrium 205
Artemis **57 sq.**, 29 *sq.*, 49, 63, 81, 110, 125, 131, 153, 159 *sq.*, 203, **p. 50**
Asklēpios *v.* Aesculāpius
Astartē **106**, 70, 108
Asteria 59
Astraeus 44
Atalanta 160, **p. 123**
Atē 14
Athamās 163
Athēnā **35 sq.**, 32, 116, 136, 179, 183, 186, 215, **p. 33**
Atlās **142**, 129, **p. 102**
Atreus 130 *sq.*
Atropos 118

Augeās 140
augurēs **207**, 19
Aurōra *v.* Ēōs
Auxō 115
Avia Lārvārum 213

Bacchae 86
Bacchus **85 sq.**, 218, **p. 74**
Bear 63
Bellerophōn *v.* Bellerophontēs
Bellerophontēs **133**, 36, 58, **p. 105**
Bellōna 116, **p. 89**
Bona Dea **201**, 199, **p. 160**
Boreās **44**, 166, **p. 38**
Brīsēis **178**, 181, **p. 141**
Brontēs 21
Būsīris 142

Cabīrī 33
Cācus 141
Cadmus **123**, 62, 166, 168, **p. 96**
cādūceüs v. kērykeion
Calaïs 166
Calchās 131
Calliopē 114
Calydonian hunt 159 *sq.*
Calypsō **182 sq.**, 185, **p. 142**
Camēnae 191
Capaneus 171 *sq.*
Carmenta 191
Carpō 115
Castalia 114
Castor 134 *sq.*, **p. 106**
Cecrops 150, **p. 122**
Celeüs 97
Centaurī **77 sq.**, 68 *sq.*, 139, 147, 156, **p. 62**
Centaurs v. Centaurī
Cēpheus 128, **p. 102**
Cerberus **7**, 143, **p. 8**
Cercōpes 145
Cercyōn 151
Cerēs **94**, 217, **p. 75**
Cerynean hind 139
Cētō 69

INDEX

Chalkeia 38
Charis **113**, 33, 105
Charites **112 sq.**, 30, 105
Charōn 7, **p. 8**
Charybdis **71**, 185, **p. 61**
Chimaera 133, **p. 105**
Chīrōn **78**, 139, 161
Chrȳsāōr 36
Chrȳseïs 178, **p. 141**
Chrȳsēs 178
Chytroi 3
Cicones 184
Cilix 123
Circē **185**, 60, **p. 143**
Clēmentia 214
Clīō 114
Clōthō 118
Clymenē 54
Clytaemnēstra **131**, 134
Clytiā 54
Cōcȳtus 6, **p. 7**
Concordia 214
Cōnsuālia 198
Cōnsus 198
Corē 95 *sq.*
creation of man 34
Creōn **137**, 165, 168, **p. 116**
Cretan bull **62**, 141, 152
Creūsa 150
Cromyonian sow 151
Cronus **21**, 30, 94, 198, **p. 29**
Cupīdō 111, **p. 86**
Cybelē **81**, 30, 58, **p. 51**
Cyclōpes **20**, 21, 33, 36, 184, **p. 30**
Cycnus 145

Daimones **10**, 12 *sq.*, 188, 191
Damastēs 151
Danaē **128**, 24, **p. 102**
Danaïdes 127
Danaüs 126 *sq.*, **p. 102**
Dea Mūta, Tacita 213
Deī Parentēs 9
Dēianīra 146 *sq.*
Dēidamīa 156

Deimos **116**, 105
Deinō 42
Dēlia 50
Delphīnia 49
Delphȳnē 50
Dēmētēr **94 sq.**, 24, 217, **p. 75**
Dēmophoōn (son of Celeüs) 97
Dēmophoōn (son of Thēseus) 157
Desire v. Pothos
Despoina 98
Diāna 203, **p. 50**
diēs parentālēs 3
Dikē **115**, 14, 30
Diomēdēs (son of Arēs) 141
Diomēdēs (son of Tydeus) 179 *sq.*, **p. 141**
Diōnē 29, 105, **p. 32**
Dionȳsia **87 sq.**, 95
Dionȳsus **85 sq.**, 32, 48, 77, 153, 200, **p. 74**
Dioscūrī **134 sq.**, 124, 156, **p. 106**
Diovis 23
Dircē 124, **p. 96**
Dīs Pater **101**, 217
Discordia 116
Dīthyrambus 88
Dīus Fidius 209
dreams **4**, 1, 48, 102, 149, 172
Dryades **80**, 83
Dryops 83

eagle **25**, 28, 34
earthquakes **73**, 22
Ēgeria 191
Elaphēbolia 57
Ēlectra 131
Eleusinia **95**, 98
Ēlysium **8**, 123, **p. 9**
Endymiōn 61
Enȳō (Bellōna) 116, **p. 89**
Enȳō (one of the Graeae) 42
Ēōs **63 sq.**, 44, **p. 51**
Epaphus 126, **p. 102**
Epicastē **168**, 170
Epigonī **174**, 167

Equīria 205
Eratō 114
Erechtheus **38**, 44, 150, **p. 33**
Erichthonius **38**, 99
Erīnyes **41**, 131, 174, **p. 34**
Eriphȳlē 171
Eris 116
Erōs **110 sq.**, 105, **p. 86**
Erymanthian boar 139
Erythēa 141
Eryx 141
Eteoclēs 170 *sq.*, **p. 133**
Ethiopians 49, 128, 133
Euandros *v.* Evander
Euanthēs 92
Eumaeus 186
Eumenides 41, **p. 34**
Eunomiā **115**, 30
Euphrosynē 113
Eurōpa **62**, 29, 123, **p. 51**
Eurus 44
Euryclēa 186
Eurygania 170
Eurynomē **113**, 32
Eurystheus **137**, 130, 143
Eurytus 144
Euterpē 114
Evander **199**, 191

Fāta 118
Fates v. Fāta
Fauna **201**, 199
Faunus 199 *sq.*
Febris 214
Fērālia 3
Fēriae Latīnae 209
Fērōnia 201
fētiālēs 209
Fidēs 209, 214
flāminēs 206, 211
flāminica 211
Flōra 202 *sq.*, **p. 160**
Flōrālia 202
Fōns, Fontus 191
Fordicīdia 213

forms of worship 15 *sq.*
Fortūna **120**, 214, **p. 92**
Furies v. Erīnyes

Gaea, Gē **99**, 24, 38
Galatēa 70
Gamēlia 56
Ganymēdā 28
Ganymēdēs 28, **p. 32**
Geniī **188**, 209
Gēryonēs 141, **p. 117**
Giants v. Gigantes
Gigantes **20**, 36, **p. 29**
Glaucus 69, **p. 61**
gorgoneion 35
Gorgones **36**, 41 *sq.*, 128, **p. 33**
Gorgons v. Gorgones
Graces v. Charites
Graeae 42, **p. 33**
Grātiae *v.* Charites
grave worship 3

Hādēs **100 sq.**, 95 *sq.*, 98, 116, 128, 131, 143, 172, **p. 76**
Haemōn 169
Halios Gerōn **69**, 146
Hamadryades 80
Harmonia **123**, 105
Harpies v. Harpȳiae
Harpȳiae **43 sq.**, 48, 166, **p. 38**
haruspicina 19
Hēbē **28**, 143, **p. 32**
Hecatē **59 sq.**, 96, 165, **p. 51**
Hectōr 180 *sq.*, **p. 142**
Helen **131**, 29, 107, 134 *sq.*, 156, 179, **p. 103**
Helieia 54
Hēlios **54**, 62, 96, 141, 164, 185
Hellē 163, **p. 128**
Heōsphoros 63
Hēphaestus **32 sq.**, 28, 38 *sq.*, 181, 197, **p. 32**
Hērā **56**, 24, 28 *sq.*, 32 *sq.*, 49, 126, 136 *sq.*, 143, 147, 161, 165, **p. 32**
Hēraklēs *v.* Herculēs

INDEX

Herculēs **136 sq.**, 20, 29, 58, 162, 216, **p. 116**
Hermaphrodītus 107, **p. 86**
Hermēs **45 sq.**, 25, 52, 65, 110, 126, 136, 216, **p. 38**
Hermionē 131, **p. 103**
heroes **122 sq.**, 8, 13
Hersē 38
Hesperides 142, **p. 117**
Hestiā 67
Himeros 111
Hippocrēnē **36**, 114
Hippodamīa (daughter of Atrax) 156, **p. 122**
Hippodamīa (daughter of Oenomaūs) 130, **p. 103**
Hippolytē **155**, 141, **p. 117**
Hippolytus 155, **p. 122**
Hippomedōn 171
Hippomenēs 160
Honōs 214
Hōrae **115**, 30
human sacrifice **2**, 26, 51, 163, 193, 203
Hyacinthus 50, **p. 50**
Hyades 90, **p. 74**
Hyakinthia 50
Hygēa 103
Hyllus 147
Hyperboreī 49
Hypermnēstrā 127
Hypnos 101, **p. 77**

Iacchus, **86**, 95, **p. 74**
Iasiōn 97
Iāsō 103
Īdās 135, **p. 106**
idea of divinity 12 *sq.*
Īlīthyia 56 *sq.*
Inachus 126
incubātiō 4
Indigetēs **190**, 204
Inferī 9
Īnō **70**, 123, 163, 183, **p. 61**
Īō 126

Iocastē **168**, 170, **p. 133**
Iolāus 138
Iolē **144**, 147
Iōn 150
Īphigenīa 131, **p. 103**
Iphitus 144
Irēnē **115**, 14, 30
Īris 65, **p. 51**
Īsis 218
Isles of the Blessed 8
Ismēnē 170
Isthmia 72
Isthmian Games v. Isthmia
Itonians 145
Ixīōn 77 *sq.*, **p. 62**

Jānus **194 sq.**, 189, 191, **p. 159**
Jāsōn 161 *sq.*, **p. 128**
Jūnō **211 sq.**, 28, 188, 207, 216, **p. 32**
Jūnōnēs 188
Juppiter **207 sq.**, 23, 28, 189, **p 30**
Jūturna 191
Juventās 207

Karneia 50
Kēres **116**, 3
kērykeion **45**, 65

Labdacus 168
labyrinth 153
Lachesis 118
Lāertēs 186, **p. 143**
Laestrȳgones 185, **p. 142**
Lāius 168 *sq.*
Lamios 145
Lāomedōn 28
Lapithae **77**, 156, **p. 62**
Lara 213
Lārentālia 213
Larēs 189
Larunda *v.* Lara
Lārvae **3**, 188
Lātōna 29
laurel 51, 53
Lēda **134**, 29, **p. 106**

Lemurēs **3**, 188
Lemūria 3
Lēnaea 88
Lernaean Hydra 138, **p. 116**
Lēthē 6, **p. 8**
Lētō **49**, 29, 57, 125, **p. 49**
Leucotheā **70**, 183, **p. 61**
Līber 200
Lībera 200
Lībertās 214
Libitīna 216
Lichās 147
Linus 137
Lōtophagī 184
Lower World **7**, 6, 41, 60, 98 *sq.*, 100 *sq.*, 129, 132, 142 *sq.*, 147, 156, 185, 213
Lūcifer 63
Lūcīna 212, **p. 165**
lūdī **210**, 198, 202, 217
Lūna 55
Lupercālia 199
Lupercī 199
Lyaeus 88, **p. 74**
Lycāōn 26, **p. 32**
Lycians 49, 133
Lycomēdēs 157
Lycūrgus 91
Lycus 124
Lynceus 127 *sq.*

Ma **58**, 30, 85, 218
Machāōn 103, **p. 78**
Maenades 86
Māgna Māter 218
Māia **25**, 45, 47, 197
Mānēs **9**, 188, **p. 9**
Mānia 213
Marathonian bull 152
Mārs **204 sq.**, 212, **p. 160**, **p. 89**
Marsyās 79, **p. 62**
Māter Mātūta 203
Mātrālia 203
Mātrōnālia 212
Mēdēa **164 sq.**, 60, 152, 161, **p. 122**

Meditrinālia 207
Medūsa **36**, 128
Megara 137
Meleager 159 *sq.*, **p. 123**
Melicertēs 70, **p. 61**
Melkart **70**, 149
Melpomenē 114
Memnōn 64
Mēnē 61
Menelāus **131**, 179, 182, **p. 103**
Menestheus 157
Mēnios 140
Mercurius **216**, 47, **p. 38**
Mētis **30**, 39
Mīlaniōn 160
Minerva **215**, 211, **p. 33**
Mīnōs **62**, 8, **p. 9**
Minotaur v. Mīnōtaurus
Mīnōtaurus **152 sq.**, 62, 158, **p. 51**
Minyās 91
Mithrās 218
Mnēmosynē 114
Moerae **118**, 30, 159, 162
moon **55 sq.**, 12, 28 *sq.*, 135, 155, 165, 203
Mūsae **114**, 30, 52 *sq.*, 191, **p. 86**
Muses v. Mūsae
Myrmidons 180
Mysteries **95**, 59, 89, 98, 218

Nāiades 80, **p. 62**
Naiads v. Nāiades
Narcissus 96, 101, **p. 75**
Nausicaa 184
necromancy 4
nectar 28
Nekysia 3
Nemean lion 138
Nemeseia **119**, 3
Nemesis **119**, 135
Nephelē **163**, 77
Neptūnālia 193
Neptūnus 193, **p. 61**
Nēreïdes **70**, 12, **p. 61**
Nereïds v. Nēreïdes

INDEX

Nēreus 69, **p. 60**
Nessus 147
Nestor **180**, 182, **p. 141**
nightmare **1**, 169
Nīkē **36**, 14, 24, 40, 104
Nile 76
Niobē **125**, 130, **p. 96**
Notus 44
Numa 191, 205
Nymphae **80**, 12, 47, 48, 58, 86, 90
Nymphs v. Nymphae

Ōceanīnae 96
Ōceanus **68**, 96, **p. 60**
Ōcypetē 43
Odysseus 182 *sq.*, **p. 142**
Oedipūs 167 *sq.*, **p. 133**
Oeneus 146, 159, 171
Oenomäus 130, **p. 103**
Oenopiōn 92
Ōgygia 183
omens v. haruspicīna
Omphalē 145, **p. 117**
Opālia 195
Opicōnsīvia 195
Ops 198
oracles **52**, 19, 25, 99, 102, 149, 172
Orcus 213
Orēades 80
Orestēs 131, **p. 103**
orgies **86**, 218
Ōriōn **63**, 57, **p. 50**
Ōrīthyia 44
Orpheus 114, **p. 87**
Oschophoria 88, 154

Palaemōn 70, **p. 61**
Palēs 202 *sq.*, **p. 160**
Palīlia 202
Palladia 35
Pallās 152
Pallas Athēnā v. Athēnā
Pān 83 *sq.*, **p. 74**
Panacēa 103
Panathēnaia 38

Pandarus 179, **p. 141**
Pandōra 34, **p. 33**
Pandrosos 38
Paniōnia 72
Parcae 118, **p. 92**
Paris 107, 131, 179, **p. 103**
Parthenopaeus 171
Pāsiphaē 62
Patroclus **180 sq.**, 2, **p. 142**
Pāx 214
Pēgasus **133**, 36, **p. 105**
Peithō 105
Peliās 161 *sq.*, **p. 128**
Pelops 130, **p. 103**
Penātēs **189**, 196
Pēnelopē **183**, 186, **p. 142**
Pentheus 91, **p. 74**
Pephrēdō 42
peplus 35 *sq.*
Periphētēs 151
Persa 164
Persēides 29
Persēis 62
Persephonē **98**, 24, 101, 106, 156, **p. 75**
Persēs 59
Perseus **128**, 35, 133, 136 *sq.*, **p. 102**
personifications **103 sq.**, 14, 99, 214
personifications of towns 99
Phaeāces 183
Phaedra **155**, 157
Phaëthōn 54, **p. 50**
Philoctētēs 147, **p. 117**
Philoetius 186
Phīneus 166, **p. 128**
Phlegra 20
Phlegyās 78, **p. 62**
Phobos **116**, 105
Phoebus *v.* Apollō
Phoenīx **123**, 62
Pholus 139
Phorcys 69
Phōsphorus 63
Phrixus 163, **p. 128**

N

Pietās 214
Pīrithoüs **156**, 78, **p. 122**
Pittheus 151
Pityokamptēs *v.* Sinis
Plēiades **63**, 25
Plūtō 101
Plūtus **97**, 115, **p. 75**
Podalīrius 103
Poeās 147
Pollux **134 sq.**, 39, 166, **p. 106**
Polybus 168
Polydeukēs *v.* Pollux
Polymnia 114
Polynīcēs 170 *sq.*, **p. 133**
Polypēmōn 151
Polyphēmus **184**, 70, **p. 142**
pomegranates **56**, 96
Pōmōna 200, **p. 160**
pontificēs **192**, 190, 196
Portūnus 195
Poseidōn **72 sq.**, 37 *sq.*, 98, 128, 150 *sq.*, 183 *sq.*, 193, **p. 61**
Pothos 111
prayer **17**, 15, 41
Priam 107, 180, **p. 142**
Priāpus 92, **p. 75**
Procrūstēs 151
Proetus 91
Promētheus **34**, 39, 142, **p. 33**, **p. 159**
Prōserpina **200**, 24, 217, **p. 75**
Prōteus 69, **p. 60**
Psȳchē **111**, 5, 48
Pudīcitia 214
purification **17**, 15, 16, 27, 51
Pyanepsia **154**, 50
Pyladēs 131
Pyriphlegethōn 6, **p. 8**
Pȳthia 52
Pȳthia 50
Pȳthōn 50, **p. 49**

Quīnquātrūs 205
Quirinālia 206
Quirīnus 206

religiō 16
Remus 205
rēx sacrōrum 194
Rhadamanthus **62**, 8
Rhēa **30**, 58, 81, 94, 198, **p. 32**
river gods **76**, 12, 192
Rōbīgus 202
Rōmulus 205 *sq.*

Sabāzius 85
sacrifices **15 sq.**, 41, 101, 121
Saēturnus *v.* Sāturnus
Salii 205 *sq.*
Salūs 214
Sarāpis 218
Sāturnālia 198
Sāturnus 198, **p. 29**
Satyrī **82**, 12, 79, 93, **p. 74**
Satyrs v. Satyrī
Scīrōn 151
Scylla **71**, 185, **p. 61**
Selēnē **61**, 29, 55, 83
Semelē **90**, 24, 123, **p. 74**
Semnai **41**, 170
serpent **4**, 20, 23, 38, 97, 102 *sq.*, 123, 133, 135, 137, 188
Sibylline books **215**, 193, **p. 169**
Sīlēnī 79
Silvānus 200, **p. 160**
Sinis 151
Sīrēnes 185, **p. 143**
Sirens v. Sīrēnes
Sīrius 63
Sīsyphus 132, **p. 104**
Sōl *v.* Hēlios
Solymī 133
souls **1 sq.**, 10, 43, 48, 116, 188 *sq.*
souls in animal form 4
Spartī **123**, 137, 168
Spēs 214
Sphinx 169
spirits of growth **81 sq.**, 199 *sq.*
spolia opīma 209
Staphylus 92
stars 63

Steropēs 21
Strophius 131
Stymphalian birds 139
Styx 6 *sq.*, **p. 7**
Summānus 208
sun **49 sq.**, 12, 21, 61 *sq.*, 148, 155, 164, 204
Syleus 145
Symplēgades 166
Synoikiā 154

taeniae **16**, 111 *sq.*
Tantalus 129, **p. 102**
Tartarus **8**, 21, **p. 9**
Telamōn 179
Tēlemachus **182**, 186, **p. 142**
Tēlephassa 62
Tellūs **99**, 213, **p. 166**
Terminus 209
Terpsichorē 114
Terra Māter *v.* Tellūs
Tēthys 68, **p. 60**
Thalīa (a Grace) 113
Thalīa (a Muse) 114
Thallō 115
Thanatos 101, 111
Thargēlia 50 *sq.*
Themis **115**, 14, 30, 118
Thersander 174
Thēseus **150 sq.**, 58, 72, 141, 143, 170, 173, **p. 122**
Thesmophoria 97
Thetis **70**, 32, 178 *sq.*, 181, **p. 61**
Thrīnaciā **54**, 185
thunderstorms **20 sq.**, 12, 130, 207 *sq.*
Thyestēs 130, **p. 103**
Thyiades 86
Tiberīnus 192
Tīresiās 170, 185
Tītānes **21**, 89, **p. 30**
Titans v. Tītānes
Tīthōnus 64, **p. 51**
tragedy 88
tribunal of the dead 8

Trīnacria *v.* Thrīnāciā
Triptolemus 97, **p. 75**
Trītōn 69, **p. 61**
Trivia 59
Trophōnius 102
Trōs 28
Tubilūstrium 205
Tychē 120 *sq.*, **p. 92**
Tydeus **171 sq.**, 179
Tyndareüs 134
Typhōeus 22, **p. 30**
Tȳphōn *v.* Typhōeus

Ulixēs *v.* Odysseus
Ulysses v. Odysseus
Ūrania 114
Ūranus **24**, 108, **p. 31**

Vējovis 208
Venus 216, **p. 85**
vēr sacrum 204
Vertumnus **200**, 203, **p. 160**
Vesta **195 sq.**, 189, **p. 159**
Vestālia 196
Victōria *v.* Nīkē
Vīnālia 207
Virtūs 214
vittae 16
Volcānus 197, **p. 32**

water **68 sq.**, 17, 191 *sq.*
wind **43 sq.**, 12, 184
wolf 26, 51, 205

Zagreus 89
Zephyrus **44**, 65, **p. 38**
Zētēs 166
Zēthus 124
Zeus **20 sq.**, 32 *sq.*, 36, 45, 56 *sq.*, 90, 96, 105, 113 *sq.*, 118, 124, 126, 128 *sq.*, 132, 134, 136 *sq.*, 163, 178 *sq.*, 183, 185, **p. 30**
Zeus *Asterios* 62
Zeus *Chthonios v.* Hādēs
Zeus *Laphystios* 163

Announcement.

THE STUDENTS' SERIES OF LATIN CLASSICS.

UNDER THE EDITORIAL SUPERVISION OF

ERNEST MONDELL PEASE, A.M.,
Leland Stanford Junior University,

AND

HARRY THURSTON PECK, Ph.D., L.H.D.,
Columbia College.

This Series will contain the Latin authors usually read in American schools and colleges, and also others well adapted to class-room use, but not as yet published in suitable editions. The several volumes will be prepared by special editors, who will aim to revise the text carefully and to edit it in the most serviceable manner. Where there are German editions of unusual merit, representing years of special study under the most favorable circumstances, these will be used, with the consent of the foreign editor, as a basis for the American edition. In this way it will be possible to bring out text-books of the highest excellence in a comparatively short period of time.

The editions will be of two kinds, conforming to the different methods of studying Latin in our best institutions. Some will contain in the introductions and commentary such a careful and minute treatment of the author's life, language, and style as to afford the means for a thorough appreciation of the author and his place in Latin literature. Others will aim merely to assist the student to a good reading knowledge of the author, and will have only the text and brief explanatory notes at the bottom of each page. The latter will be particularly acceptable for sight reading, and for rapid reading after the minute study of an author or period in one of the fuller editions. For instance, after a class has read a play or two of Plautus and Terence carefully, with special reference to the peculiarities of style, language, metres, the methods of presenting a play, and the like, these editions will be admirably suited for the rapid reading of other plays.

The Series will also contain various supplementary works prepared by competent scholars. Every effort will be made to give the books a neat and attractive appearance.

The following volumes are now ready or in preparation: —

CAESAR, Gallic War, Books I-V. By HAROLD W. JOHNSTON, Ph.D., Professor in the Indiana University.

CATULLUS, Selections, based upon the edition of Riese. By THOMAS B. LINDSAY, Ph.D., Professor in Boston University.

CICERO, Select Orations. By B. L. D'OOGE, A.M., Professor in the State Normal School, Ypsilanti, Mich.

CICERO, De Senectute et de Amicitia. By CHARLES E. BENNETT, A.M., Professor in the Cornell University.

CICERO, Tusculan Disputations, Books I and II. By Professor PECK.

CICERO, De Oratore, Book I, based upon the edition of Sorof. By W. B. OWEN, Ph.D., Professor in Lafayette College. *Ready.*

CICERO, Select Letters, based in part upon the edition of Süpfle-Böckel. By Professor PEASE.

EUTROPIUS, Selections. By VICTOR S CLARK, Lit.B., New Ulm High School, Minn. *Ready.*

GELLIUS, Selections. By Professor PECK.

HORACE, Odes and Epodes. By PAUL SHOREY, Ph.D., Professor in the Chicago University. *Nearly Ready.*

HORACE, Satires and Epistles, based upon the edition of Kiessling. By JAMES H. KIRKLAND, Ph.D., Professor in Vanderbilt University. *Ready.*

LIVY, Books XXI and XXII, based upon the edition of Wölfflin. By JOHN K. LORD, Ph.D., Professor in Dartmouth College. *Ready.*

LIVY, Book I, for rapid reading. By Professor LORD.

LUCRETIUS, De Rerum Natura, Book III. By W. A. MERRILL, Ph.D., Professor in the University of California.

MARTIAL, Selections. By CHARLES KNAPP, Ph.D., Professor in Barnard College.

NEPOS, for rapid reading. By ISAAC FLAGG, Ph.D., Professor in the University of California. *Ready.*

NEPOS, Selections. By J. C. JONES, A.M., Professor in the University of Missouri.

OVID, Selections from the Metamorphoses, based upon the edition of Meuser-Egen. By B. L. WIGGINS, A.M., Professor in the University of the South.

OVID, Selections, for rapid reading. By A. L. BONDURANT, A.M., Professor in the University of Mississippi.

PETRONIUS, Cena Trimalchionis, based upon the edition of Bücheler. By W. E. WATERS, Ph.D., President of Wells College.

PLAUTUS, Captivi, for rapid reading. By GROVE E. BARBER, A.M., Professor in the University of Nebraska.

PLAUTUS, Menaechmi, based upon the edition of Brix. By HAROLD N. FOWLER, Ph.D., Professor in the Western Reserve University. *Ready.*

PLINY, Select Letters, for rapid reading. By SAMUEL BALL PLATNER, Ph.D., Professor in the Western Reserve University. *Ready.*

QUINTILIAN, Book X and Selections from Book XII, based upon the edition of Krüger. By CARL W. BELSER, Ph.D., Professor in the University of Colorado.

SALLUST, Catiline, based upon the edition of Schmalz. By CHARLES G. HERBERMANN, Ph.D., LL.D., Professor in the College of the City of New York. *Ready.*

SENECA, Select Letters. By E. C. WINSLOW, A.M.

TACITUS, Annals, Book I and Selections from Book II, based upon the edition of Nipperdey-Andresen. By E. M. HYDE, Ph.D., Professor in Lehigh University.

TACITUS, Annals, Book XV. By J. EVERETT BRADY, Ph.D., Professor in Smith College.

TACITUS, Agricola and Germania, based upon the editions of Schweizer-Sidler and Dräger. By A. G. HOPKINS, Ph.D., Professor in Hamilton College. *Ready.*

TACITUS, Histories, Book I and Selections from Books II-V, based upon the edition of Wolff. By EDWARD H. SPIEKER, Ph.D., Professor in the Johns Hopkins University.

TERENCE, Adelphoe, for rapid reading. By WILLIAM L. COWLES, A.M., Professor in Amherst College. *Ready.*

TERENCE, Phormio, based upon the edition of Dziatzko. By HERBERT C. ELMER, Ph.D., Assistant Professor in the Cornell University. *Ready.*

TIBULLUS AND PROPERTIUS, Selections, based upon the edition of Jacoby. By HENRY F. BURTON, A.M., Professor in the University of Rochester.

VALERIUS MAXIMUS, Fifty Selections, for rapid reading. By CHARLES S. SMITH, A.M., College of New Jersey. *Ready.*

VELLEIUS PATERCULUS, Historia Romana, Book II. By F. E. Rockwood, A.M., Professor in Bucknell University. *Ready.*

VERGIL, Books I-VI. By E. Antoinette Ely, A.M., Clifton School, and S. Frances Pellett, A.M., Binghamton High School, N.Y.

VERGIL, The Story of Turnus from Aen. VII-XII, for rapid reading. By Moses Slaughter, Ph.D., Professor in Iowa College. *Ready.*

VIRI ROMAE, Selections. By G. M. Whicher, A.M., Packer Collegiate Institute. *Ready.*

LATIN COMPOSITION, for college use. By Walter Miller, A.M., Professor in the Leland Stanford Jr. University. *Ready.*

LATIN COMPOSITION, for advanced classes. By H. R. Fairclough, A.M., Professor in the Leland Stanford Jr. University.

HAND-BOOK OF LATIN SYNONYMS. By Mr. Miller.

A FIRST BOOK IN LATIN. By Hiram Tuell, A.M., Principal of the Milton High School, Mass., and Harold N. Fowler, Ph.D., Western Reserve University. *Ready.*

EXERCISES IN LATIN COMPOSITION, for schools. By M. Grant Daniell, A.M., formerly Principal of Chauncy-Hall School, Boston. *Ready.*

A NEW LATIN PROSE COMPOSITION. By M. Grant Daniell, A.M. *Ready.*

THE PRIVATE LIFE OF THE ROMANS, a manual for the use of schools and colleges. By Harriet Waters Preston and Louise Dodge. *Ready.*

GREEK AND ROMAN MYTHOLOGY, based on the recent work of Steuding. By Karl P. Harrington, A.M., Professor in the University of North Carolina, and Herbert C. Tolman, Ph.D., Professor in Vanderbilt University. *Ready.*

ATLAS ANTIQUUS, twelve maps of the ancient world, for schools and colleges. By Dr. Henry Kiepert, M.R. Acad. Berlin. *Ready.*

Tentative arrangements have been made for other books not ready to be announced.

LEACH, SHEWELL, & SANBORN,
Boston, New York, and Chicago.

www.ingramcontent.com/pod-product-compliance
Lightning Source LLC
Chambersburg PA
CBHW020238170426

43202CB00008B/127